MW00510760

Growing in CHRiST®

Early Childhood Teacher Guide

CONCORDIA PUBLISHING HOUSE · SAINT LOUIS

Jesus Teaches about God's Kingdom

NEW TESTAMENT 3

Concordia Publishing House
3558 S. Jefferson Ave., St. Louis, MO 63118-3968
1-800-325-3040 • www.cph.org

Lesson 1 copyright © 2006, 2016 Concordia Publishing House
Lesson 2 copyright © 2010, 2016 Concordia Publishing House
Lessons 3–6, 9, 11, and 12 copyright © 2007, 2016 Concordia Publishing House
Lesson 7 copyright © 2016 Concordia Publishing House
Lessons 8, 10, and 13 copyright © 2008, 2016 Concordia Publishing House

All rights reserved. Unless specifically noted, no part of this publication may be reproduced, stored in a retrieval system, or transmitted, in any form or by any means, electronic, mechanical, photocopying, recording, or otherwise, without the prior written permission of Concordia Publishing House.

The purchaser of this publication is allowed to reproduce the marked portions contained herein for use with this curriculum. These resources may not be transferred or copied to another user.

Lessons 1, 5, 6, and 9 written by Marlene Krohse in consultation with Lorraine Groth
Lesson 2 written by Jeanette Dall in consultation with Lorraine Groth
Lessons 3, 4, 11–13 written by Jessemyn Pekari in consultation with Lorraine Groth
Lesson 7 written by Lorraine Groth
Lessons 8 and 10 written by Chris Behnke in consultation with Lorraine Groth

Edited by Lorraine Groth

Scripture quotations are from the ESV Bible® (The Holy Bible, English Standard Version®), copyright © 2001 by Crossway Bibles, a publishing ministry of Good News Publishers. Used by permission. All rights reserved.

Manufactured in the United States of America

Growing in Christ® is published by Concordia Publishing House. Your comments and suggestions concerning this material are appreciated. Email us at sundayschool@cph.org.

Contents

Introduction

For the New User

Early Childhood is a nonreader level for children in preschool and kindergarten. It includes a Teacher Guide, Teacher Tools, and Student Pack.

Features of the Teacher Guide

- Easy-to-use, four-step weekly lesson plans
- A weekly Bible study on the first page of each lesson to help the teacher prepare
- Reproducible Activity Pages in each lesson for student and teacher use
- Age-appropriate ways to teach the Bible story and apply it to young lives
- Themed snack suggestions in every lesson
- Songs, wiggles-out rhymes, and ways to involve children in active learning
- Quarterly supply list at the back of the book
- Perforated pages to make team teaching or small-group/large-group teaching easier

Teacher Tools

This packet provides the following resources for effective teaching:

- **Posters** (teaching aids and Bible story posters)
- **Storytelling Figures** (four pages of figures for telling the Bible stories)
- **Bible Story Background Tent** (two background scenes to use with the figures)
- **Attendance chart**
- **CD** (recordings of hymns, songs, Bible Words, and Bible stories; melody-line scores for all music on the CD; Activity Pages, Resource Pages, and a list of student Bible Words in PDF format; and song lyrics in RTF format)

Student Pack

You will need one for each child. This packet includes the following materials:

- **Student Book** that contains Lesson Leaflets and Craft Pages and a list of the Bible Words at the back of the book to send home with the children
- **Sticker Pages** (three pages with perforated sections for each lesson)
- **CD** with songs, hymns, catechism songs, and Bible memory words songs

Additional Teaching Helps

Call 1-800-325-3040 for subscription and cost information to order the following:

- *Little Ones Sing Praise* (LOSP) songbook
- *Sing & Wonder* (S&W) songbook
- *Wiggle & Wonder: Bible Story Rhymes and Finger Plays* (W&W)
- *Happy Times*, a magazine for young children
- **Puppets**—find an assortment of fun puppets online at cph.org; Jelly can be used interchangeably with Sprout
- **Restickable glue stick**—provides repeat use in attaching storytelling figures to backgrounds (order online at cph.org, or find in the office supply section of a local store)
- **Church Year Worship Kit**—a great resource for teaching children about the Church Year (includes a Leader Guide, an altar poster with paraments and more, prayer posters, and a CD)

Early Childhood Format

Young children need a safe environment with predictable routines and the same caring adults each week to feel secure. For this reason, we recommend letting them learn in their own space, separate from the rest of your program, where they can relax, play, and engage in age-appropriate activities.

You can still make choices in how you organize your Sunday School session and space. Choose the option that works best for your program.

Option 1

This format works well if you just have one group of children with one teacher (or a teacher and helper). It is a traditional, self-contained classroom where the teacher does all the activities with the whole group of children. If this format suits you, then begin with the "Welcome Time" learning activities and work through the lesson as it is written, adapting the materials to fit your time frame and children's needs. Encourage parents to do the Activity Page with their child before they go to their own Bible class or other activity. This helps children transition into the classroom more easily. It also gives parents a better understanding of what the lesson will be about so they can talk later with their child about what he or she learned.

Make copies of Activity Page Fun before class so each parent or helper has one. Set these out with copies of the Activity Page and the other supplies they'll need.

If your class session is under an hour, omit the "Welcome Time" activities and start with the "Opening" ritual or Bible story.

Option 2

If you have a large number of children in your early childhood program, try a large-group, small-group format. In this approach, children gather in their own class-rooms or designated space to do the "Welcome Time" learning activities.

These learning activities serve two purposes: they help children transition into the classroom, and they activate prior knowledge, building interest and readiness for what children will learn in the lesson. Encourage parents to do the Activity Page with their child during this time before going to their own Bible study session.

When it is time to begin, all children in your early childhood program gather with their teachers in one location for the opening worship ("Gathering in God's Name"). Stay in this location to have a teacher tell the Bible story to the whole group, or have children go back to their own classrooms again for the Bible story ("God Speaks"), told by their classroom teacher.

The "We Live" life-application activities can be done in two ways. Teachers can do these activities in their classroom with their small group of children. Or you can set up each activity as a station. Children divide into small groups and rotate to these sta-tions or sites. Then all preschoolers through kindergartners come back together again for the "Closing."

Abbreviations

LSB = *Lutheran Service Book* (Concordia Publishing House, 2006)

LOSP = *Little Ones Sing Praise* (Concordia Publishing House, 1989)

W&W = *Wiggle & Wonder* (Concordia Publishing House, 2012)

S&W = *Sing & Wonder* (Concordia Publishing House, 2015)

TG = *Teacher Guide*

Preparing the Lesson

Jesus Preaches on the Mount

Matthew 5:1–12

Key Point

Because Jesus was poor, hungry, sorrowful, hated, and rejected for our sake, God forgives our sins and blesses us with all good gifts, especially life with Him forever.

Law/Gospel

In this world, I suffer and struggle because of my sin. **Jesus offers comfort, mercy, and grace through faith in Him and gives me eternal riches and blessings.**

Context

Jesus has been baptized and tempted. He has heard the news of the arrest of John the Baptist. He has called His first disciples. Now, He begins His ministry in earnest, teaching to great crowds of people. This portion of Matthew is commonly known as the Sermon on the Mount.

Commentary

Jesus has power to heal, but the greatest gift He gives suffering humanity is His Word. Those He heals of one disease will succumb to another. Those He raises from the dead will die again. But those He brings to faith will have comfort now and untold blessings in the world to come.

The Greek word *makarios* ("blessed") is a "declaration of blessedness" upon the person who is in communion with God through Jesus Christ. There are many beatitudes in the Bible, including fifteen in Luke's Gospel (1:45; 6:20–22; 7:23; 10:23; 11:27–28; 12:37–38, 43; 14:14–15; and 23:29).

In the kingdom of God, the hungry are filled, the mourning rejoice, the last become first, and God chooses the foolish to shame the wise and learned.

The Beatitudes are Christological—all of them apply to Jesus. He was poor and hungry, a man of sorrows acquainted with grief. Yet it was for the joy set before Him that He endured the cross, despising its shame. He now sits at the right hand of God. He was hated, despised, rejected, cast out, beaten, spat upon, and crucified. Yet now, risen from the dead, He has a name that is above all other names, at which every knee shall bow in heaven and on earth and every tongue confess that Jesus Christ is Lord to the glory of the Father.

The Beatitudes are Gospel. Do not turn them into Law. They are descriptive, not prescriptive. They show what life is like in Christ: things may be bad for you in this life, but in the life to come, you will have joy forevermore.

Finally, the Beatitudes are both spiritual and physical in their meaning. Luke says, "Blessed are the poor"; Matthew says, "Blessed are the poor in spirit." Both are true. Generally speaking, Christianity has advanced most rapidly among the poor, the hungry, the outcast, the hopeless of society. In the United States, where studies have shown that most people living below the official poverty line have two cars and a television, we must take a more spiritual application.

The statement "Blessed are those who hunger" is talking about those who are spiritually hungry, but it can also apply to those who are physically hungry. Jesus fed the five thousand, and they were filled. The Greek word *chortazo* ("fill") is used in both places. This vivid word derives from *chortos* ("grass") and indicates a state of being full like a cow that has eaten so much it couldn't possibly hold another bite. By grace we hunger after the things of God, and He fills us to the brim. It is likewise with those who weep.

Everyone in the world has trouble and sorrow, and God uses those troubles to draw people to Himself through Christ. In the arms of our suffering Savior, we find comfort and consolation. At the same time, our deepest grief is over our sins. Yet Jesus Christ takes our sins upon His own body on the cross and gives us the same beatitude He gave the thief: "Today you will be with Me in Paradise" (Luke 23:43).

To hear an in-depth discussion of this Bible account, visit cph.org/podcast and listen to our Seeds of Faith podcast each week.

Lesson 1

Jesus Preaches on the Mount

Matthew 5:1–12

Connections

Bible Words
Rejoice and be glad.
Matthew 5:12
God . . . has blessed us in
Christ with every spiritual
blessing. Ephesians 1:3

Faith Words
Blessed, blessing

Hymn
How Sweet the Name of
Jesus Sounds (*LSB* 524;
CD 2)

Catechism
Apostles' Creed: First and
Second Articles

Liturgy
The Benediction

Take-Home Point
God blesses me through
Jesus.

1 Opening (15 minutes)

Welcome Time

What you do: Before class, set up two activity areas. In one, put out copies of Activity Page 1 and crayons. Make copies of Activity Page Fun (below and on CD) for parents or classroom helpers. Adjust talk as necessary.

In the other activity area, set out play dough and other embellishments (e.g., buttons, pipe cleaners, gems). *Option:* Use a handheld device to record each child telling about some of the blessings he or she has fashioned.

Play the CD from your Teacher Tools. As the children arrive, greet each one. Give them a sticker to put on the attendance chart.

Say Hi, [Madelyn]. I'm glad you're here. I wonder . . . do you know what a blessing is? Today, we're going to learn about some blessings God gives us.

Direct children to the tables where you have the activities. Encourage parents or caregivers to stay and do the welcome activity with their child.

Activity Page Fun Get a copy of Activity Page 1 to show your child.

Say God blesses us with many good things! Point to the pictures on the left-hand side of the page. Here are blessings God gives us. Name the items. Draw a line from each blessing to the person or people who need that blessing. What are some blessings God gives you? When your child matches the picture of Jesus to the bottom scene, talk about how Jesus died on the cross for us to give us forgiveness and a home in heaven with Him.

© 2016 Concordia Publishing House. Reproduced by permission. Available on the Teacher CD.

MATERIALS NEEDED

1 Opening	2 God Speaks	3 We Live	4 Closing
Teacher Tools Attendance chart & CD	**Teacher Tools** CD	**Student Pack** Lesson Leaflet 1 Craft Page 1 Stickers	**Teacher Tools** CD
Student Pack Attendance stickers	**Student Pack** Lesson Leaflet 1 Craft Page 1 (optional)	**Other Supplies** Sprout Grapes or fish crackers Paper Plus supplies (optional)	**Student Pack** Take-home materials
Other Supplies Activity Page 1 (TG) Play dough Embellishments (optional) Resource Page 1 (TG, optional)	**Other Supplies** Sprout Picture of Jesus Items that depict blessings (optional)		

Active Learning Encourage the children to use the play dough and embellishments to make some of God's blessings (food, clothing, etc.). Show them how to make a cross. Remind them that we have all our blessings because of Jesus, who died on the cross for us and rose again.

Use your classroom signal when it is time to clean up, or sing a cleanup song (Resource Page 1). Cue the children to gather them for your opening.

Say Come and learn of Jesus, our Savior and our Friend.
Come and worship Jesus; His love is without end.

Gathering in God's Name

What you do: Begin with this opening. To teach about the Church Year, use the materials in the Church Year Worship Kit (see the introduction for more information).

Sing "We Are in God's House Today" (*LOSP*, p. 12; CD 15) or another opening song

Invite the children to say the Invocation and Amen with you. Tell them "Amen" is the special word they get to say at the end of prayers, hymns, and others parts of the church service.

Say We are going to learn about the blessings God gives us through Jesus.

Begin In the name of the Father and of the Son and of the Holy Spirit. Amen.

Offering Have a child bring the offering basket forward. Sing an offering song.

Pray Dear Father, thank You for all the blessings You give us through Your Son, Jesus. Thank You most of all for sending Jesus to be our Savior. In His name we pray. Amen.

Celebrate Birthdays, Baptism birthdays, and special occasions

Teacher Tip

If you do not do the opening activities, be sure to introduce the concept of blessing or being blessed. Stress that blessings are gifts, not something we earn by being good. God blesses us with good things for the sake of Jesus, who made us right with God through His death and resurrection.

2 God Speaks (20 minutes)

Story Clue

What you do: Children identify with puppets. Use Sprout to build a bridge from what children know to what they will learn. Sprout enters, crying.

Teacher: Hi, Sprout! What's the matter? Why are you crying?

Sprout: I feel really sad today. My cousin Lily was going to come for a visit, but now she can't. We were going to go to the zoo together. And she was going to stay overnight. I haven't seen her for a long time. I miss her! (*Sniff*)

Teacher: What a disappointment! I'm sure Lily feels bad too. (*Sprout nods head.*) I know you are sad, Sprout. Jesus knows how you feel too! The Bible tells us that Jesus felt sad and even cried sometimes.

Sprout: Really? I didn't know Jesus got sad too. I'm glad He knows how I feel, and I know Jesus loves me. But I'm still sad that Lily can't come.

Teacher: It's okay to feel sad. But also remember that Jesus is with you. In our Bible story today, Jesus says those who mourn, or are sad, are blessed through Him. He will help you when you are sad, and He promises to take away all your sadness in heaven. Jesus teaches about *lots* of other blessings, or good things, that we have through Him too. Let's find out what they are.

Bible Story Time

What you do: Listen to the story on CD (20), or use the following script. If you tell the story, ring a bell to cue the children. Practice their line before listening to the story. Add an action to the "I'm blessed too" phrase (e.g., have children give themselves a hug). Hold up a picture of Jesus on the "Jesus said" parts.

Option: If you have an extra Craft Page, cut apart the six pictures and mount them on separate sheets of construction paper. Show each picture as indicated to give children a visual cue for the story. Or, instead of using the Craft Page, gather items or pictures of the items to show. For this option, you'll need a toy crown, a tissue box, a food item, a cross, a picture of a baptismal font (take one on your tablet device), and a picture of a child singing.

Say **Today, you will hear about special blessings from God. A blessing is a special favor or gift God gives because He loves us. Every time you hear the [chime/bell], I want you to say, "I'm blessed too." Let's practice.** Do so. Then begin CD, or tell the story.

Say **People followed Jesus everywhere He went. They wanted Him to heal their hurts and make them better. They wanted to hear Him teach about God's love. When Jesus saw the big crowd of people, He went up a mountainside and sat down. Then He began to teach. Jesus told them about special gifts, or blessings, God gives His people.**

Jesus said, "Blessed are the poor in spirit, for theirs is the kingdom of heaven." Show crown. **The poor in spirit are people who are sorry for their sins. They know they need Jesus to be their Savior. Jesus promises life in heaven to all who believe in Him. Jesus says, "Blessed are the poor in spirit."** *Children: I'm blessed too!*

Next, Jesus said, "Blessed are those who mourn, for they shall be comforted." Show tissue box. **Many things make us sad. Jesus understands how we feel because He was sad too. He even let people hurt Him on the cross so that He could pay for our sins. Jesus promises to be with us and help us when we are sad. He promises to take away all our sadness in heaven. Jesus says, "Blessed are those who mourn."** *Children: I'm blessed too!*

Next, Jesus said, "Blessed are the meek, for they shall inherit the earth. Blessed are those who hunger and thirst for righteousness, for they shall be satisfied." Show food. **God blesses us with many good things because of Jesus. He gives us food, clothes, a place to live, and people to love us. Best of all, He forgives our sins for Jesus' sake and gives us a wonderful home in heaven. Jesus says, "Blessed are the meek."** *Children: I'm blessed too!*

Next, Jesus said, "Blessed are the merciful, for they shall receive mercy. Blessed are the pure in heart, for they shall see God." Mercy is kindness we get even when we've been bad and don't deserve it. It's when our mom gives us a big hug after we were naughty and says, "I forgive you." Mercy is God's gift to us. It is not something we deserve. God showed mercy to us by sending Jesus to take the punishment for our sins on the cross. Show cross. **He helps us show love and mercy to others. Jesus says, "Blessed are the merciful."** *Children: I'm blessed too!*

Next, Jesus said, "Blessed are the peacemakers, for they shall be called sons of God." Sin makes God angry and sad. It brings trouble and sad-

Key Point

Because Jesus was poor, hungry, sorrowful, hated, and rejected for our sake, God forgives our sins and blesses us with all good gifts, especially life with Him forever.

Growing in CHRIST.

ness and even death into our world. But God loves us. He sent His Son, Jesus, to take away our sins. Jesus gives us God's forgiveness and peace. God makes us His children in Holy Baptism. *Show baptismal font.* Jesus says, "Blessed are the peacemakers." *Children: I'm blessed too!*

Then Jesus said, "Blessed are those who are persecuted for righteousness' sake, for theirs is the kingdom of heaven." Sometimes, people make fun of us for believing in Jesus or going to church. They make us feel bad. Jesus understands how we feel. People picked on Him and hurt Him, even though He never did anything wrong. Then He died on the cross to pay for our sins. He did that for us so that we can live with Him in heaven.

Even when we are sad or lonely, Jesus is with us and blesses us. He takes care of us. No matter what happens, we can rejoice and be glad. *Show child singing.* Someday, we will live with Jesus forever in heaven, where there will be no more hurts and no more sin. Jesus says, "Blessed are those who are persecuted." *Children: I'm blessed too!*

Bible Story Review

What you do: Show Lesson Leaflet 1 to the children. Use these questions to review the story and check for understanding. Then hand out Lesson Leaflet 1 and crayons to the children. For an active review, use the action poem.

Ask **What is Jesus telling the people?** He is teaching them about God's love and telling them they are blessed.

What are some of the blessings Jesus gives you? Let children tell.

Direct children to find the sidebar pictures in the big picture. Give them time to color the pictures. On side 2, have them connect the dots and draw a blessing. Then have children stand and do the action rhyme with you.

Say **My life is full of blessings** *Spread arms open wide.*
That come from Jesus' love, *Point heavenward; hug self.*
Like parents, friends, and teachers *Look around you.*
And sunshine from above. *Hold arms toward sky.*
When Jesus died upon the cross, *Make cross with fingers.*
He took my sins away, *Pretend to wash hands.*
And that is why I can rejoice *Wave arms happily.*
And be glad every day! *Smile extra big.*

Bible Words

What you do: Open your Bible to read Matthew 5:12 and Ephesians 1:3. For younger children, teach just Matthew 5:12: "Rejoice and be glad."

Say **The Bible says, "Rejoice and be glad."**
"God . . . has blessed us in Christ with every spiritual blessing."

Ask **What are some of the blessings God gives you?** Let children tell.

Say **God gives us all these blessings through Jesus, especially forgiveness! That makes us glad! Let's say our Bible Words together.** Do so.

Sing "Rejoice in the Lord Always" (*LOSP*, p. 52). Lead children in a parade around the room as you sing, or have children stand up and sit down on each "rejoice." End with the Bible Words.

Active Learning Idea!

(3) We Live (15 minutes)

Choose the activities that work best with your class to help children grow in their understanding of what the Bible story means for their lives.

Growing through God's Word

What you do: Bring out Sprout for another talk.

Sprout: Hi, Teacher; I liked that Bible story. But what's a peacemaker?

Teacher: A peacemaker is someone who tries to get people to stop fighting.

Sprout: Oh, like when my mom tells me to share with my friend and not fight over my toys?

Teacher: Right! Your mom is being a peacemaker. I imagine she is pretty good at that too. But Jesus is the best peacemaker ever! The Bible calls Him the Prince of Peace because He died on the cross for our sins.

Sprout: I have another question. What does *merciful* mean?

Teacher: To be merciful means to be kind and loving, even when people don't deserve it.

Sprout: Uh-oh. I'm not always kind to people. I'm not a peacemaker either because I fight with Lily sometimes. Does that mean I'm not blessed?

Teacher: Sadly, Sprout, we all sin. But God blesses us through Jesus. Jesus is the only one who is perfect. It's because of Jesus' perfect life and His dying on the cross to pay for our sins that we are saved. We are not peacemakers, but Jesus is. We aren't merciful, but Jesus is. All these words describe Jesus, and all the blessings they promise are ours because of Jesus.

Sprout: Is that why Jesus said, "Rejoice and be glad"?

Teacher: Yes, that's right. Because of Jesus, we can rejoice and be glad. He forgives us, and someday we will go to live with Him in heaven.

Craft Time

What you do: Give the children Craft Page 1, stickers, and crayons to make a two-sided puzzle. Side 1 shows gifts with visual clues that stand for the blessings we have in Jesus. Side 2 has scenes that show God's blessings.

Say In our Bible story today, Jesus talks about special blessings, or gifts. Look at the gift boxes on your page. They will help us remember what these blessings, or gifts, from Jesus are. After we talk about them, you can color the bows.

Show crown gift. **What is this? The crown reminds us that Jesus makes us part of His kingdom. Let's add some jewels to make our crowns beautiful.** Give children jewel stickers to add to crown.

Show tissues gift. **Why do we use tissues? Yes, they wipe away our tears. The tissues remind us that Jesus is with us when we are sad.** Have children color the tissue paper or tape pieces of tissue to it.

Point to gift with food and family on it. **What do you see on this gift? God gives us food and clothes and many other blessings. What is your favorite blessing? God blesses us with good things because of Jesus.** Give children sticker of Jesus to add.

Growing in CHRIST.

Show gift box with cross. **What does the cross remind you of? God forgives our sins because of Jesus. He shows mercy to us because of Jesus.** Connect dots and color cross.

Point to baptismal font. **What do you see on this gift? God makes us His children in Baptism. Because He is our heavenly Father, God hears and answers our prayers. He is with us and takes care of us.** Color the shell.

Point to last gift. **What is on this gift? Give the girl a mouth to praise God. Because of Jesus, we can rejoice and be glad. God has blessed us in Jesus with every spiritual blessing. Through Him, we have forgiveness and a home in heaven. These are the best blessings of all!**

Turn the page over and point out the blessings shown on this side. Have children color the tissue in the scene of the child being comforted and give the teacher a Bible story book sticker to read to the children. Point out that the children are wearing crowns because they belong to God's kingdom through faith in Jesus. Add a dog sticker to the home scene and a baby sticker to the pastor's arm. As the children color the heart and cross, talk about how God blesses us and forgives our sins because of Jesus' death on the cross.

Cut apart the scenes on the solid lines between the gifts on side 1. Arrange the pieces of side 2 so the heart shows. The children can put this side together as a puzzle, using the heart shape as a clue.

Paper Plus option: Glue the cut-apart gifts to a piece of wide ribbon or strip of construction paper to make a mobile to hang at home.

Snack Time

Serve a simple snack, such as fish crackers or halved grapes. Talk about how it is a blessing from God.

Live It Out

Encourage children to share what they did in Sunday School today by telling the Bible Words and singing "Rejoice in the Lord Always" or "I Have the Joy" to someone at home this week.

 **4 Closing** (5 minutes)

Going Home

What you do: Send home take-home pages and crafts. Cue CD.

Sing "I Have the Joy" (*LOSP*, p. 62) or "How Sweet the Name of Jesus Sounds" (*LSB* 524; CD 2)

Say **May the Lord bless us and keep us and give us His peace. Before you leave, let's say "God blesses me through Jesus" together.** Do so.

Pray **Dear Jesus, thank You for blessing us in so many ways. Thank You for forgiving us and giving us eternal life with You. Amen.**

Reflection

Were you adequately prepared to teach this lesson? How can you adjust the lesson to better meet the special needs of the children in your class?

Liturgy Link

Use words from the Aaronic blessing in Numbers 6:24–26 to bless the children when they leave today. Tell them that these words are also said in the Benediction at the end of worship. They remind us of God's blessings on all believers.

Jesus Blesses Me

Activity Page 1 Growing in Christ® Early Childhood © 2006 Concordia Publishing House. Reproduced by permission. This page is available on the Teacher CD.

Preparing the Lesson

Jesus Teaches Us to Trust

Matthew 6:25–34

Key Point

As we seek God's kingdom through Christ, we are freed from worry, knowing we have all we need.

Law/**Gospel**

I worry about my life because I depend on myself instead of on God. **Jesus, who provided for my greatest need by paying for my sins on the cross, describes the Father's care for creation to show me His love and take away my worry.**

Context

Jesus preaches to all believers, those who are "poor in spirit" and therefore possess God's kingdom by grace, through faith (Matthew 5:1–3). He has taught His followers to pray for spiritual, heavenly blessings in the Lord's Prayer (6:5–14) and to find lasting treasure in heaven, not on earth (6:19–24). Now, He assures His disciples that the Father cares for their physical needs as well.

Commentary

Being anxious or worried is sin because it demonstrates unbelief in God's providential care. Faced with the accusation of God's Law, our sinful inclination is to deny that we have a problem with worry, but making excuses will accomplish nothing before God's judgment seat. Repentance is our only option, especially as we face the one unavoidable cause of anxiety in life: death. In fact, our preoccupation with food, clothing, health, and wealth is another sign of our unbelief.

Jesus, in His incarnation, entered our stressful, anxious existence and was "tempted as we are, yet without sin" (Hebrews 4:15). He endured hunger, homelessness, and hatred from others but never worried about food, clothing, shelter, or safety. He always had perfect faith in His Father, so He wasn't concerned in the slightest about proper medical care as He faced the cross for our sins. The Lily of the Field was thrown into the oven of God's wrath to be burned up for all of our sins of worry and care and faithlessness. Therefore, He has overcome our greatest anxiety by dying to "destroy the one who has the power of death," Satan (Hebrews 2:14). He has delivered us from the slavery of the fear of death by promising us everlasting resurrected life with Him.

Now the same Jesus authoritatively tells us, "Do not be anxious, but simply trust in Me." His promises relieve our anxieties and reveal a gracious heavenly Father who just can't wait to bless us. His analogies for this are vivid. Just picture a flock of geese tilling, sowing, waiting, and harvesting or lilies picking cotton, spinning thread, and weaving garments. Both are ridiculous! The Lord cares for them! This does not mean that we are to be lazy (see 2 Thessalonians 3:10), but as we live out our vocations, we have no cause for worry at all.

Yet to remain free from worry, we must always put into practice Jesus' admonition: "Seek first the kingdom of God and His righteousness" (Matthew 6:33). That must be our top priority—if we can even call it a priority. What God has done and is still doing for us in Jesus Christ—the Gospel, the righteousness of God—goes beyond being a priority and actually is all in all for us. So we joyfully seek God's kingdom in Word, Sacrament, and prayer. These are far more real and enduring than the stuff of this life. Jesus bids us look to Him as the focal point of all of our life, to rest in His forgiveness, and to find in Him the secure ground of confidence for facing all of life's apparent ambiguities and anxieties.

To hear an in-depth discussion of this Bible account, visit cph.org/podcast and listen to our Seeds of Faith podcast each week.

Lesson 2

Jesus Teaches Us to Trust

Matthew 6:25–34

Connections

Bible Words
Do not be anxious about anything. Philippians 4:6

Faith Word
Trust

Hymn
How Sweet the Name of Jesus Sounds (*LSB* 524; CD 2)

Catechism
Baptism

Liturgy
Apostles' Creed: First Article

Take-Home Point
I can trust God to take care of me.

1 Opening (15 minutes)

Welcome Time

What you do: Before class, set up two activity areas. In one, put out copies of Activity Page 2A and three different colors of crayons for each child (e.g., blue, red, and green). Make copies of Activity Page Fun (below and on CD) for parents or classroom helpers. Adjust talk as necessary.

In the other activity area, set out blue, yellow, and brown play dough and bird cookie cutters.

Play the CD from your Teacher Tools. As the children arrive, greet each one. Give them a sticker to put on the attendance chart.

Say Hi, [Nicholas]. It's good to see you! I wonder . . . what's your favorite bird? What is special about it? Did you know that Jesus says birds can teach us about God's care? I wonder how? We'll find out today.

Direct children to the tables where you have the activities. Encourage parents or caregivers to stay and do the welcome activity with their child.

Activity Page Fun Get a copy of Activity Page 2A and crayons. Point to the pictures at the top of the page. Have your child color the crayons under the bird, flower, and children, using a different color for each one. Then use the color that matches each of the pictures to draw circles around the things it needs.

Ask What do birds do? Where do flowers grow? What is your favorite one? Talk about birds and flowers. **What do children need? Today, you'll hear what Jesus said about birds and flowers and God's care. He knows just what they need, and He knows what we need too. Be sure to listen!**

© 2016 Concordia Publishing House. Reproduced by permission. Available on the Teacher CD.

MATERIALS NEEDED

1 Opening	2 God Speaks	3 We Live	4 Closing
Teacher Tools Attendance chart & CD	**Teacher Tools** Storytelling Figures 2-1 to 2-6 Background A	**Student Pack** Craft Page 2 Stickers	**Teacher Tools** CD
Student Pack Attendance stickers	**Student Pack** Lesson Leaflet 2 Stickers	**Other Supplies** Bag containing food, clothing, toys & additional items	**Other Supplies** Take-home materials
Other Supplies Activity Page 2A (TG) Brown, yellow & blue play dough Bird cookie cutters Resource Page 1 (TG, optional)	**Other Supplies** Seeds & plant Decorative bird Bird food *Jesus Teaches Us Not to Worry* Arch Book (optional)	Activity Page 2B (TG) & newsprint Trail mix & gummy worms Pinecones, yarn, bird seed & shortening Paper Plus supplies (optional)	

Active Learning Show the children how to make a nest and some eggs out of the play dough. Help them use the cookie cutter to make birds.

Say **Today, we will hear how God cares for the birds. He loves us even more and will care for us too.**

Use your classroom signal when it is time to clean up and gather for the story. Sing a cleanup song (Resource Page 1). Cue the children when it is time to gather for your opening.

Say **Come and learn of Jesus, our Savior and our Friend.**
Come and worship Jesus; His love is without end.

Gathering in God's Name

What you do: Begin with this opening. To teach about the Church Year, use the materials in the Church Year Worship Kit (see the introduction for more information).

Sing "God's a Father Kind and True" (*LOSP*, p. 30) or another song

Invite the children to say the Invocation and Amen with you. Tell them "Amen" is the special word they get to say at the end of prayers, hymns, and others parts of the church service.

Begin **In the name of the Father and of the Son and of the Holy Spirit.**
Amen.

Offering Have a child bring the offering basket forward. Sing an offering song.

Pray **Dear Lord, thank You for taking care of the birds and flowers.**
Thank You for taking care of us and giving us what we need. Amen.

Celebrate Birthdays, Baptism birthdays, and special occasions

2 God Speaks (20 minutes)

Story Clue

What you do: Have a package of flower seeds, a plant, a decorative bird, and some bird seed to show.

Ask **If this were a real bird** (show decorative bird), **what would it need?**

Say **It would need some water, a place to make a nest, and some food. It might eat food like I have here.** Show bird seed. **Or it may eat berries or worms.** Hold up package of flower seeds and shake it.

Ask **What do you think is in this package?** Accept answers. Open the package and show the seeds. **What do these seeds need in order to become a beautiful plant like this?** Show plant.

Say **Seeds need to be planted in dirt; they need water and sunshine to grow into plants.**

Ask **Do you think flowers worry about getting rain and sunshine to grow? Do you think birds worry about what to eat or where to build a nest?**

Say **In our Bible story today, Jesus says the birds and flowers teach us about God's care. Let's find out what He means.**

Teacher Tip
Young children really like to be helpful—it makes them feel useful and important. To promote this feeling, choose a different child each week to be in charge of giving the cleanup signal.

Bible Story Time

What you do: Use Background A and Storytelling Figures 2-1 to 2-6. Put the figures in your Bible, and remind the children that this is a true story from God's Word. Use a restickable glue stick (see Introduction for more information), double-sided tape, or loops of tape to attach the figures to the background when you tell the story.

Option: Show the pictures and tell the story using the Arch Book *Jesus Teaches Us Not to Worry* (CPH, 59-2245).

Say Jesus liked to teach people about God's love. We can read about the things Jesus talked about in God's Word, the Bible. Open Bible to Matthew 6.

Place Jesus (2-1) on the background. **One day, lots of people came to hear Jesus teach about God. They sat down around Him. The people had many worries. Some of them were sick, and they were afraid they would not get well. Some of the people were worried about getting enough food to eat or clothes to wear. Some of them needed a house to live in.**

Key Point

As we seek God's kingdom through Christ, we are freed from worry, knowing we have all we need.

Jesus knew that the people were worried. So Jesus told them, "Don't worry about food. Look at the birds. Place the bird (2-2) on the background. **See them flying? They are happy and safe. They don't plant seeds to grow food. They don't store away food in barns. God takes care of them! He gives them what they need. God gives the birds trees to make nests and live in.** Place tree (2-3) on the background. **God gives them food to eat.** Place worms (2-4) on the background. **You are more important to God than the birds. God takes care of you too."**

The people thought about what Jesus said. They could see that the birds had everything they needed. They had food and water and safe places to sleep. The birds did not worry about anything.

Then Jesus pointed to all the beautiful flowers growing around them. Place the flowers (2-5) on the background. **Jesus said, "Look at all the flowers in the fields. Look at all their bright colors! God takes care of the flowers.** Place rain (2-6) on the background. **God sends rain to water the flowers and the sun to help them grow. He gives them everything they need. You don't need to worry about clothes. You are more important than the flowers. God takes care of you too." When the people looked at the flowers, they could see how God took care of them.**

Then Jesus reminded the people, "Don't worry about what you will eat or what you will wear. God will take care of you. Just remember how much more special you are to God than the birds and flowers. God knows everything you need. Trust in Him to take care of you."

Jesus wanted the people to know how important they were to God and that He would give them what they needed. The things He told them are part of what we call Jesus' Sermon on the Mount.

We are all very important to God too. God takes good care of the birds and flowers, but He takes even better care of us. So we don't need to worry. God loves us so much that He sent Jesus to die on the cross for our sins. He forgives our sins for Jesus' sake. We can trust Him to take care of us.

Bible Story Review

What you do: Hand out the Lesson Leaflet 2, stickers, and crayons to each child. Help the children find and count the flowers, Jesus, and birds in the Bible art and then circle the correct number in the sidebar. Point to the picture as you review the story with these questions.

Ask **How does God take care of the birds?** Accept answers.

How does God take care of the flowers? Accept answers.

How does God take care of you? Accept answers.

Have children draw and color flowers. On side 2, they can color the pictures and place heart stickers by all the things God cares for.

Option: Ask children to name some ways God cares for us; then do the finger play "God Cares about You" (*Fingers Tell the Story*, p. 82) together.

Bible Words

What you do: Read the words of Philippians 4:6 from your Bible.

Say **The Bible says, "Do not be anxious about anything." When we are anxious, we are afraid or nervous about what will happen. We don't need to be anxious or afraid, though, because God loves us. He gives us what we need. We don't need to worry about our food or clothes or anything else. We can trust God to take care of us. Let's say the Bible Words together.** Say the verse together several times.

Option: Sing the song on the back of the leaflet to the tune of "Mary Had a Little Lamb" to reinforce that we don't need to be worried or anxious. God takes care of us and gives us what we need. Music helps children focus and remember words and concepts. Using a familiar tune makes it easier for them to concentrate on the words. Video-record the children singing the song. Send it home to parents this week.

Active Learning Idea!

Sing **God takes care of birds and flowers,** *Move hands like bird flying.*
Birds and flowers, birds and flowers;
God takes care of birds and flowers;
They don't have to worry. *Shake head no.*

God takes care of me and you, *Point to self and others.*
Me and you, me and you;
God takes care of me and you;
We don't have to worry. *Shake head no.*

After the song, say the Bible Words together again.

3 We Live (15 minutes)

Help children grow in their understanding of what the Bible story means for their lives. Choose the activities that work best with your class.

Growing through God's Word

What you do: Put items needed to live, such as a can of soup, a bottle of water, a fruit and vegetable, a child's jacket, and a small blanket (optional) in a grocery bag or your story bag. Then add some nonessential things such as a stuffed animal, a doll, a video, a book, a rock, and a popular toy.

Say **Phew! This bag is heavy. I wonder what's inside. Let's find out.** Take the items out, one by one, and place them on the table.

Ask **Do you ever worry about having the things you need? Do you see anything here that you need?** Accept answers.

Ask the children to help you separate the items into two piles. In one pile, put the things that we need to live (water, food, clothing, warmth from a blanket when it's cold). In the other pile, put things that aren't necessary, even though they may be nice to have (games, toys, videos, etc.). As you pick up each item, let a volunteer tell you into which pile to place it.

Ask **How does God take care of us?** Accept answers.

Say **God gives us a place to live, people who love us, our church and school, and many, many more things. God takes care of the birds and flowers and gives them what they need to live. God loves us much more than He loves them. He loves us so much that He sent Jesus to die for our sins. He forgives us, and He gives us a home in heaven where we will live with Jesus and all who believe in Him someday. We can trust God to care for us. He gives us what we need.**

Craft Time

What you do: Give the children Craft Page 2, stickers, scissors, and crayons or markers to make a doorknob hanger. Make a sample ahead of time for the children to look at. If you have young children, cut out the doorknob hanger and the hole for the doorknob ahead of time.

Give the page to the children. Have them cut out the hanger, cut the solid diagonal line at the top, then cut out the middle of the hanger. Give help as needed. Direct them to put the bird and flower stickers on the front of the hanger. Read the words on the hanger.

Say **"God takes care of the birds and flowers." Jesus said the birds and flowers don't worry about getting the things they need. God takes care of them.**

Turn over the hanger, and have the children color the child. Read the words.

Say **"God takes care of ME!" God loves us much more than the birds and the flowers. We don't need to worry or be afraid. We can trust God to give us everything we need.**

Show the children how the hanger fits on a doorknob. Encourage them to take it home and hang it where they can see it to remind them that God cares for them.

Paper Plus option: Copy Activity Page 2B for each child. Use it to make a classroom mural or individual mobiles. For the mural, you will need large sheets of paper or a roll of newsprint, crayons, scissors, and glue. Check with your local newspaper office. Sometimes, they give away the ends of newsprint rolls for free. Have children color and cut out the birds on Activity Page 2B, and glue them to the mural paper. Print "God cares for the birds and flowers" across the top. Hang it in the classroom to enjoy.

To make mobiles, give each child half a paper plate, crayons, scissors, and lengths of yarn for hanging the birds. Have children color and cut out the birds on Activity Page 2B. Punch holes in the birds, and string with varying lengths of yarn. Punch holes in the bottom of the paper plate to hang them from the plate or tape them in place. Print Bible Words on the plate.

Snack Time

Serve bird food today. Make a simple trail mix (pretzels, goldfish, raisins, M&M's, etc.) and add gummy worms. Talk about how God takes care of the birds and us.

Live It Out

Make bird feeders to help children learn about their stewardship of God's creation. Make one classroom feeder together, or let each child make a feeder to take home. Have wipes or water and paper towels for cleanup.

For each feeder, you will need a pinecone, a 12-inch piece of yarn, shortening, and bird seeds. Cover each pinecone with solid shortening. Then roll it in bird seed. Tie yarn to the end for hanging.

Hang a classroom feeder near a window, or tell children to hang their feeders near a window at home so they can observe any birds that visit. Talk about how God cares for the birds and flowers. One way He does that is through us.

 **4 Closing** (5 minutes)

Going Home

What you do: Send home take-home pages and crafts. Cue CD.

Sing "Thank You, Loving Father" (LOSP, p. 71; CD 13) or "How Sweet the Name of Jesus Sounds" (*LSB* 524; CD 2)

Say **God takes care of the birds and flowers, and God takes care of us. We don't need to worry. God loves us and gives us everything we need.** Lead children in saying "I can trust God to take care of me."

Pray **Dear God, thank You for Your love and care. Thank You for loving us so much that You sent Jesus to die on the cross for our sins. Help us to trust You and not worry. Amen.**

Reflection

Did the children feel a sense of love and caring as they learned about how God loves and cares for them?

Lesson 2

Directions: Color each crayon a different color. Use the color of crayon under the bird to draw a circle around the things the bird needs. Use the color of crayon under the flower to circle the things plants need. Use the color of crayon under the children to circle things that children need.

Activity Page 2A *Growing in Christ® Early Childhood* © 2010, 2016 Concordia Publishing House. Reproduced by permission. This page is available on the Teacher CD.

Activity Page 2B *Growing in Christ®* Early Childhood © 2010 Concordia Publishing House. Reproduced by permission. This page is available on the Teacher CD.

Lesson 3

Preparing the Lesson

Jesus Is Anointed

Luke 7:36–50

Date of Use

Key Point

In faith, a sinful woman lovingly anointed Jesus' feet. In faith, we grasp God's free mercy, receive the forgiveness of sins, and respond with acts of love and praise.

Law/Gospel

My sin troubles and harms me, condemning me to eternal death. **God offers His love and forgiveness to me and all sinners who call upon Him for mercy and grants me His peace.**

Context

Luke's account of Jesus' anointing differs from the other Gospels, which tell of an anointing in Bethany just days before Jesus' crucifixion (Matthew 26:6–13; Mark 14:3–9; John 12:1–8). John provides the name Mary, the sister of Martha and Lazarus, as the woman in the Bethany account.

Like the woman caught in adultery, the sinful woman in Luke's account remains unnamed. In Luke's account, Jesus uses the woman's actions to teach the Pharisees, and us, the true meaning of repentance and forgiveness. This woman is so filled with grief she does not even dare speak to Jesus. Here is a woman who offers penitent sacrifice without precondition or reserve.

Commentary

Offering sacrifices does not save you by your own merit. Like the tax collector in the temple, the woman of the city knew something Simon the Pharisee did not. She treated Jesus with honor, while Simon showed dishonor. Her sorrow was great, while his was little. She had nothing to say before the Son of God; he had a lot to say and was rather critical at that. She knew where sin puts us all, namely, at the point of abject filth, dirt, and dung. In her sacrifice, her position behind Jesus and at or under His feet, coupled with her not daring even to speak in the presence of the holy Lord, makes a confession of who Jesus is and what He should have received from Simon.

Our forgiveness in Christ does not lie in the manner of our penitence, but it comes from Christ alone because He desires to save us. Yet Christ is also pleased when we show how important and necessary He is for our salvation by being sorry for our sins and recognizing our Savior as the only source of forgiveness and help that we can possibly have. That homage is mandated by our Lord and Savior— homage that we, with all the saints, shall render eternally before God.

This sinful woman forgets her past and follows Jesus, who has made her to be a new creation. So it is with us. We who have been forgiven and remade now remain alive in Christ and dead to sin. And on the Last Day, we, too, shall be raised from dishonor to glory, from mortality to immortality.

To hear an in-depth discussion of this Bible account, visit cph.org/podcast and listen to our Seeds of Faith podcast each week.

Lesson 3

Jesus Is Anointed

Luke 7:36–50

Connections

Bible Words
We love because [God] first loved us. (1 John 4:19)

Faith Word
Offering

Hymn
How Sweet the Name of Jesus Sounds (*LSB* 524; CD 2)

Catechism
First Commandment

Liturgy
Offering

Take-Home Point
Because Jesus loves me, I can show love for others.

1 Opening (15 minutes)

Welcome Time

What you do: Before class, set up two activity areas. In one, put out copies of Activity Page 3 and crayons. Make copies of Activity Page Fun (below and on CD) for parents or classroom helpers. Adjust talk as necessary.

In the other activity area, set out scented items (e.g., perfume, vanilla, cinnamon, cloves, hand lotion, baby powder). If you wish to do the option, have a cloth to cover the items.

Play the CD from your Teacher Tools. As the children arrive, greet each one. Give them a sticker to put on the attendance chart.

Say Hi, [Willow]. Did you go to church yet? Did you give an offering? Today, we're going to hear about someone who gave Jesus a special offering.

Direct children to the tables where you have the activities. Encourage parents or caregivers to stay and do the welcome activity with their child.

Activity Page Fun Get a copy of Activity Page 3. Point to Jesus.

Ask Who is this? Yes, it's Jesus. How much does Jesus love us? Spread arms wide. **Jesus loves us so much that He died on the cross to pay for our sins!** Point to woman. **This woman is happy Jesus loves her. I wonder, what will she do to show Him that? Listen when your teacher tells the Bible story to find out what she did. You can tell me about it later.**

On the back of the page, trace around your child's hand. Talk about ways we show love for Jesus in what we say and do in response to His love for us.

© 2016 Concordia Publishing House. Reproduced by permission. Available on the Teacher CD.

MATERIALS NEEDED

1 Opening	2 God Speaks	3 We Live	4 Closing
Teacher Tools Attendance chart & CD	**Teacher Tools** Poster A	**Student Pack** Craft Page 3 Stickers	**Teacher Tools** CD
Student Pack Attendance stickers	**Student Pack** Lesson Leaflet 3	**Other Supplies** Offering plate Cologne bottle Construction paper heart 3 × 5 cards Yarn (optional) Popcorn, orange slices, or spice cookies Paper Plus supplies (optional)	**Student Pack** Take-home materials
Other Supplies Cologne Other scented items & cloth Activity Page 3 (TG) Resource Page 1 (TG, optional)	**Other Supplies** Gift box with cross inside Hand lotion Throw pillows		

Active Learning Have the children sniff each of the scented items you set out. *Option:* Hide them under a cloth and leave the top off the items. Have the children smell each item; then tell what it is.

Ask **What smell do you like the best? Today, we will hear about a woman who used spices and smells such as these to show love to Jesus.**

Use your classroom signal when it is time to clean up, or sing a cleanup song (Resource Page 1). Gather children for your opening routine and the Bible story with this movement activity, leading them to where they will sit.

Say **I can clap and clap my hands,**
Clap my hands, clap my hands,
I can clap and clap my hands,
Thank You, God, for hands.
I can shake and shake my hands . . .
I can use my hands to hug . . .
I can fold my hands to pray . . .
Now let's use our hands and fold them in our lap as we sit down.

Gathering in God's Name

What you do: Begin with this opening. To teach about the Church Year, use the materials in the Church Year Worship Kit (see the introduction for more information).

Sing "We Are in God's House Today" (*LOSP*, p. 12; CD 15) or another opening song

Invite the children to say the Invocation and Amen with you. Tell them "Amen" is the special word they get to say at the end of prayers, hymns, and others parts of the church service.

Begin **In the name of the Father and of the Son and of the Holy Spirit. Amen.**

Offering Have a child bring the offering basket forward. Sing an offering song.

Pray **Dear Jesus, You love us all the time, no matter what. You paid for our sins on the cross. We thank and praise You, dear Jesus, for Your great love. Amen.**

Celebrate Birthdays, Baptism birthdays, and special occasions

2 God Speaks (20 minutes)

Story Clue

What you do: Bring a gift box or a bag with a cross or crucifix inside.

Ask **What is your favorite birthday present?** Let the children take turns telling.

Say **God gives us many gifts. And we don't even have to wait for our birthday to open them! Today, I brought a present with me.** Show box. **It will help us remember the best gift God gives us. Let's open it and see what it is.** Take out cross.

Teacher Tip

If you have children who are hyperactive, involve them in a learning activity that lets them use their sense of touch. These sensory activities often have a calming effect.

Ask What is it? Let children tell. **Who does a cross remind us of?** Jesus!

Say Jesus died on the cross to take away our sins. What Jesus did is very special. He did it because He loves us and wants us to live with Him forever in heaven someday. That is the best gift ever! It makes us feel thankful. In today's true story from the Bible, a woman is so thankful for Jesus' love that she wanted to do something special for Jesus. Let's listen and find out what she did.

Bible Story Time

What you do: You will need Poster A. Use a piece of paper to cover the woman. Have some hand lotion for the children to smell. Some children may be willing to have you put lotion on their hands. Check ahead of time for skin sensitivity to perfumed products before doing this. Bring throw pillows for the children to sit on so they can act out how people ate in Jesus' day.

Say A man named Simon invited Jesus and His friends for supper. The people sat on pillows and ate at tables that were near the ground. Show children Poster A with the woman covered up. Give the children pillows, and have them pretend they are reclining at the table and eating with Jesus. Simon had lots of good food for Jesus and his other guests to eat.

A woman who lived in the town heard that Jesus was there. This woman had done many wrong things. People said she was bad. They called her a sinful woman. The woman wasn't invited to the party, but she came anyway. She knew that Jesus loved her and forgave her. She wanted to do something special for Him to show that she loved Him too.

Ask What do you think she did? Accept suggestions; then show all of Poster A.

Key Point

In faith, a sinful woman lovingly anointed Jesus' feet. In faith, we grasp God's free mercy, receive the forgiveness of sins, and respond with acts of love and praise.

Say The woman came and stood near Jesus' feet. She started crying. Big, fat tears dripped onto Jesus' feet. She was crying because she was so thankful for Jesus' love and forgiveness. Then the woman took a special jar of wonderful-smelling perfume that cost lots and lots of money. Let children smell the hand lotion.

She poured the perfume on Jesus' feet so they smelled wonderful too. Rub some lotion on the hands of the children who would like some. Then she dried Jesus' feet with her long hair. Simon saw what the woman did. He wondered, "How can Jesus let this sinful woman touch Him? She has done so many wrong things!"

Jesus told Simon, "This woman knows that she has done many bad things. But I love her. I have forgiven her sins. That makes her thankful and glad!" Then Jesus told the woman, "Go in peace."

Jesus loves us too. He loves us so much that He died on the cross to pay for our sins. Jesus was pleased with the way the woman showed her love for Him. Jesus is pleased when we show that we love Him too. The Bible says we show love for Jesus when we love others.

Bible Story Review

What you do: Show Poster A. Check for understanding by asking the questions. Then hand out Lesson Leaflet 3 and crayons or markers.

Ask What is the woman doing? She is putting perfume on Jesus' feet and

Growing in CHRiST.

drying them with her hair.

What does Jesus tell the woman? Your sins are forgiven.

What has Jesus done for you? He died on the cross to pay for our sins.

How does that make you feel? Accept answers.

Direct attention to the sidebar pictures on side 1 of the leaflets. Ask what the woman put on Jesus' feet. Have children circle and color it.

On side 2, have children color the perfume in the bottle, and then connect the dots on the offering plate. Talk about ways we can say thank You to God for His love (e.g., give an offering, help someone).

Bible Words

What you do: Read the Bible Words from 1 John 4:19 in the Bible. Use the action poem to help the children learn the words.

Say The Bible says, "We love because [God] first loved us." In our Bible story, the woman knew she was a sinner. But she also knew Jesus loved her and forgave her sins. Because she was thankful for His love, she wanted to show her love for Him by doing something special.

We think and say and do bad things too. But God loves us and forgives us for Jesus' sake. He makes us His children and helps us to show love for others. Let's say our Bible Words together. Divide children into two groups to say the Bible Words, or sing "We Love" (*LOSP,* p. 54).

Group 1: We love *(clap, clap)* **because [God] first loved us.**

Group 2: We love *(clap, clap)* **because [God] first loved us.**

Group 1: We love *(clap, clap)***.**

Group 2: We love *(clap, clap)***.**

Together: We love *(clap, clap)* **because [God] first** *(clap)* **loved** *(clap)* **us** *(clap)***.**

3 We Live (15 minutes)

Help children grow in their understanding of what the Bible story means for their lives. Choose the activities that work best with your class.

Growing through God's Word

What you do: Ask your pastor if you can borrow an offering plate from church to show the children, or take the children to church to look at the offering plates. If you cannot use a real offering plate, use your offering basket from Sunday School or take a picture of your church's offering plate on your smartphone and show it to the children. Have a bottle of cologne and a heart cut from construction paper. Show the offering plate to begin your discussion.

Ask Who knows what this is? Many of the children will find it fascinating to look closely at something they see just briefly each week, so give them time to examine it. **What do we use it for?** Let the children tell.

Say **God sent Jesus to be our Savior. Because of Jesus, God forgives our sins. He gives us good things like food and clothes and our parents and**

a home. **God's love makes us thankful. One way we say thank You to God is by giving Him an offering in church.** Talk about, and then act out, how the offering is collected in church and brought to the altar to say thank You to Jesus for His love.

The woman in our story was thankful that Jesus loved her. She wanted to do something special for Him.

Ask **What offering did she bring Jesus?** Let the children tell; then place the cologne bottle in the offering plate (or show it to the children).

Say **She gave Jesus expensive perfume.** Place the heart in the offering plate (or show it). **The woman showed love to Jesus because He first loved her by forgiving her sins.**

Jesus has saved us from our sins too. He makes us His children in Baptism and through His Word. Because Jesus loves us, we are joyful and can show love too.

Ask **Can we pour perfume on Jesus' feet?** No. **What are some things we *can* do to say thank You to Jesus for His good gifts?** Let the children tell.

Say **We can bring an offering to Sunday School and church.** Talk about what our offerings do to bless people. **We can show love by being kind to others. What are some ways we can do that?** Discuss ideas (e.g., share toys, help Mom with jobs at home, give someone a hug). **We give gifts or offerings to God to say thank You to Him for loving us and sending Jesus to be our Savior.**

Craft Time

What you do: Give the children their Craft Pages, stickers, and crayons. Make a project ahead of time to show the children. Cut out the square for the basket first. Cut slits in the corners and overlap them to make a basket shape. Tape the corners in place. Tape strip for the handle to the basket. Color the offering pictures before cutting them apart.

Supply 3 × 5 cards for the children to draw pictures of additional offerings.

Say **Today, we are going to make offering baskets.** Have the children cut off the basket bottom and handle. Point to the dot-to-dot cross on the basket. **What is this? Yes, a cross. The cross reminds us that Jesus died to pay for our sins. Jesus' love makes us thankful!** Have children connect the dots and color the cross. Show them how to assemble the basket.

Ask **What can we put in our offering basket to say thank You to Jesus?** Point to the strip of six pictures. **We cannot pour perfume on Jesus' feet to show our love. But Jesus tells us in the Bible that when we show love by doing things for other people, we are showing love to Him too. What are these children doing?**

Talk about how the children are giving an offering to Jesus by what they are doing (e.g., singing in the choir, folding towels) and ways we can do that too. Give the children stickers of a dish, flowers, towel, and money to add to the appropriate pictures. Have them draw a singing mouth on the child in the choir.

Give them stickers of a cross and a cross with a heart to add to the card with the Bible Words rebus. Help them "read" the Bible Words. When the children are finished, have them put the cards in their offering baskets and say, "Thank You for loving and forgiving me, Jesus. I love You too."

Say Jesus was happy that the woman showed love for Him by what she did. Jesus is happy when we show love for others too. He is happy when we sing and pray and give Him thanks. But do we always do that? No. Sometimes we don't want to share our toys. Sometimes we are hurtful. Sometimes we don't want to give Jesus our money.

Ask Does Jesus still love us? Yes! Jesus' love is so big that He died on the cross for all the times we say and do wrong things. He came back to life and will take us to heaven to live with Him there someday.

Paper Plus option: Make sachets by putting a drop of perfume on a cotton ball and wrapping it in a fabric square. Tie with ribbon or yarn.

Snack Time

Serve a food that smells good, such as hot popcorn, orange slices, or spice cookies.

Live It Out

Draw around each child's hands onto poster paper. Inside the hands, have the child draw (or dictate) ways he or she can show love for others this week. *Option:* If you made sachets, suggest that the children choose someone to give their sachet to. Tell them to share the Bible story with this person and say, "Jesus loves you and so do I."

Faith in Action!

4 Closing (5 minutes)

14, 2

Going Home

What you do: Send home take-home pages and crafts. Cue CD.

Sing "There Is a Name I Love to Hear" (*LOSP,* p. 44; CD 14) or "How Sweet the Name of Jesus Sounds" (*LSB* 524; CD 2)

Say Jesus loves us so much that He died for us. Because Jesus loves us, we can show love for others. Let's say that together: Because Jesus loves me, I can show love for others. Lead children in repeating this.

Ask What are some ways we can show love? Accept answers.

Say We thank Jesus when we give offerings at church or show love to others by doing kind things. We thank Jesus by singing and praying to Him. Let's tell Jesus thank You now!

Pray Dear Jesus,* thank You* for dying on the cross.* Thank You* for always loving us.* Help us to tell others* about Your great love.* Amen.* Have children echo each phrase at the asterisk.

Reflection

Offerings aren't just the money we give in church. Everything we do in faith according to the Ten Commandments, to the glory of God, or for the benefit of our neighbor is an offering. Did your children tell about ways they can thank God for all that He does for them?

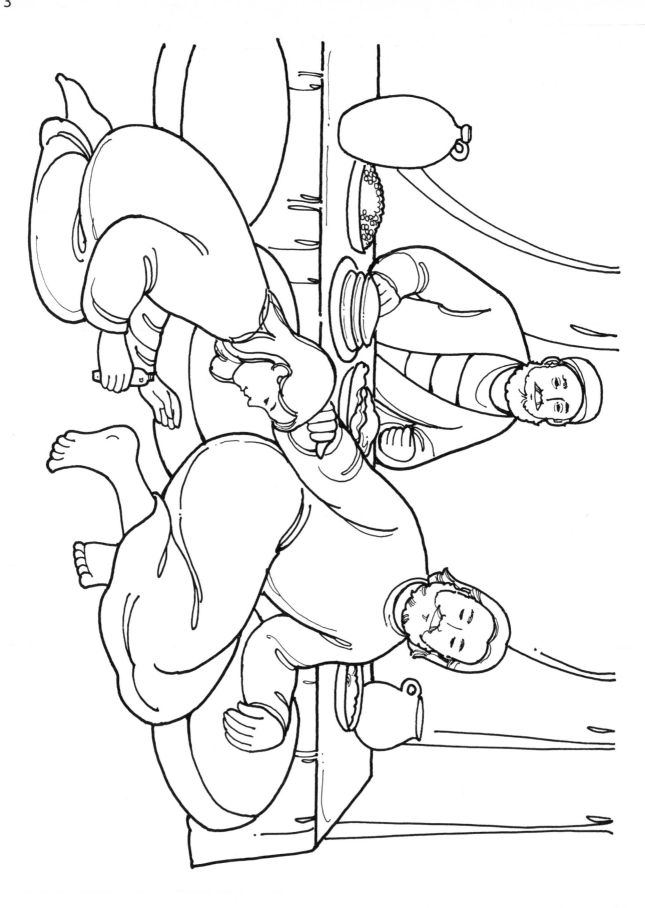

We love because [God] first loved us. 1 John 4:19

Activity Page 3 Growing in Christ® Early Childhood © 2007, 2016 Concordia Publishing House. Scripture: ESV®. Reproduced by permission. This page is available on the Teacher CD.

Preparing the Lesson

Jesus Feeds Five Thousand

John 6:1–14

Key Point

In His love, God promises to care for all our physical and spiritual needs and gives us the greatest treasure: His Son and the gifts of forgiveness, life, and salvation.

Law/**Gospel**

Like the disciples, my faith is weak, and I lack trust in God to give me all good things. **For the sake of His Son, Jesus, God promises to provide for all my needs and gives me the gift of faith to believe in Jesus as my Savior and receive eternal life through Him.**

Context

John 6 begins with the feeding of the five thousand and ends with Jesus' statement, "I am the bread of life," and Peter's confession, "Lord, to whom shall we go? You have the words of eternal life. . . . You are the Holy One of God." Peter's words are associated with the Lord's Supper. The three synoptic Gospel records of the account of the feeding of the five thousand speak of the time following the execution of John the Baptist and the Galilean beginning of Jesus' journey to Jerusalem.

Commentary

Millions go hungry, get sick, and experience enmity and death. Apart from the goodwill of God the Father and the love of Christ, we have no hope. Were we the captains of our own destinies, we would surely flounder upon the reefs. One day, we shall all depart this life.

God feeds the hungry, whether Jew or Gentile. God makes some kind of society, government, and conflict resolution possible in the face of overwhelming sin and self-interest. God loves us that much!

Yet God does not grant a general amnesty from sin apart from Jesus Christ. The gift of abundant earthly food is best understood as pointing to the bread of life, Christ, who fills your soul eternally. God steers all good things in your life that you might find Christ and help lead others to Him—not only as the bread giver of the here and now but also as the eternal living bread of heaven.

As Jesus' feeding miracles helped strengthen the individual faith of the disciples after the gruesome death of John the Baptist, so His daily feeding and strengthening of your faith will sustain you through all trouble. In Christ, you receive all the necessary physical and spiritual energy to run the race and keep your eyes on the goal of receiving the crown of eternal life.

To hear an in-depth discussion of this Bible account, visit cph.org/podcast and listen to our Seeds of Faith podcast each week.

Lesson 4

Jesus Feeds Five Thousand

John 6:1–14

Connections

Bible Words
God will supply every need. Philippians 4:19

Faith Word
Provide

Hymn
How Sweet the Name of Jesus Sounds (*LSB* 524; CD 2)

Catechism
Lord's Prayer: Fourth Petition

Apostles' Creed: First Article

Take-Home Point
God gives me what I need.

1 Opening (15 minutes)

Welcome Time

What you do: Before class, set up two activity areas. In one, put out copies of Activity Page 4A and crayons. For a tactile component, provide sequins or cake sprinkles to glue on the cookies. Make copies of Activity Page Fun (below and on CD) for parents or classroom helpers. Adjust talk as necessary.

In the other activity area, set out play dough and toy baking utensils (e.g., muffin cups, mini rolling pins, dishes) or a Go Fish card game.

Play the CD from your Teacher Tools. As the children arrive, greet each one. Give them a sticker to put on the attendance chart.

Say **Hi, [Henry]. What's your favorite thing to eat? Where does it come from?** Use this welcome time to build relationships with children.

Direct children to the tables where you have the activities. Encourage parents or caregivers to stay and do the welcome activity with their child.

Activity Page Fun Show Activity Page 4A to your child.

Say **This tray has lots of cookies. Let's count them together. Draw some more cookies. How many are there now?** Let child draw more and recount them. Then have child color and decorate the cookies.

Say **You helped make cookies for [eight] people. In your Bible story today, Jesus takes one little boy's lunch and does something special with it. Listen carefully to find out what He did. You can tell me about it later.**

© 2016 Concordia Publishing House. Reproduced by permission. Available on the Teacher CD.

MATERIALS NEEDED

1 Opening	2 God Speaks	3 We Live	4 Closing
Teacher Tools Attendance chart & CD	**Teacher Tools** Storytelling Figures 4-1 to 4-7 Background A	**Teacher Tools** Poster B	**Teacher Tools** CD
Student Pack Attendance stickers	**Student Pack** Lesson Leaflet 4 & stickers	**Student Pack** Craft Page 4 Stickers	**Student Pack** Take-home materials
Other Supplies Activity Page 4A (TG) Toy baking utensils Play dough Cake sprinkles or sequins; Go Fish card game (optional) Resource Page 1 (TG, optional)	**Other Supplies** Picnic basket or lunch bag & snack Apron (optional) Activity Page 4B (TG) *What's for Lunch?* Arch Book (optional)	**Other Supplies** Activity Page 4C (TG) Goldfish crackers Napkins & plastic sandwich bags Paper Plus supplies (optional)	

Active Learning Encourage the children to use the play dough and toy utensils to pretend to make food for company.

Ask   Who is coming to your house? What will you make for them to eat? Will you make a little food or a lot? In today's Bible story, Jesus makes a little boy's lunch into lots of food to feed many people.

Option: Play Go Fish. Tell children to listen for "fish" in the Bible story.

Use your classroom signal when it is time to clean up, or sing a cleanup song (Resource Page 1). Cue the children when it is time to gather.

Sing   Come and listen to God's Word, to God's Word, to God's Word. Come and listen to God's Word, from His book, the Bible.

Gathering in God's Name

What you do: Begin with this opening. To teach about the Church Year, use the materials in the Church Year Worship Kit (see the introduction for more information).

Sing   "We Are in God's House Today" (*LOSP*, p. 12; CD 15) or another song

Invite the children to say the Invocation and Amen with you. Tell them "Amen" is the special word they get to say at the end of prayers, hymns, and others parts of the church service.

Begin   In the name of the Father and of the Son and of the Holy Spirit. Amen.

Offering   Have a child bring the offering basket forward. Sing an offering song.

Pray   Thank You, God, for giving us everything we need—our families and food and clothes. Thank You especially for forgiving us for Jesus' sake. Amen.

Celebrate   Birthdays, Baptism birthdays, and special occasions

2 God Speaks (20 minutes)

Story Clue

What you do: Bring a child's picnic basket or a lunch bag with a snack inside (e.g., crackers, apple, and cookies).

Say   Today, I brought a lunch with me. I thought I'd go to the park to eat it. Would you like to see what I brought? Take out the items one at a time and talk about how good they will taste. **My family might come eat with me.**

Ask   Do you think they'll like what I brought? Do you think I have enough food for them? Accept answers. **What if I invite all the children in Sunday School to eat lunch with me? Do you think there is enough food for all of us?** Expect a variety of answers. **What if I invite all the people in our church family? Would my lunch be big enough to feed all of us?**

Say   No, my little lunch wouldn't feed that many people. Shake head no. **I would need more food to feed that many. In our Bible story today, Jesus takes a little boy's lunch and does something special. He provides lots and**

lots of food for a big crowd of hungry people. But He does it in a special way. Let's listen to the story and find out how Jesus did this.

Bible Story Time

What you do: Use Background A and Storytelling Figures 4-1 to 4-7. Put the figures in your Bible, and remind the children that this is a true story from God's Word. Attach the figures to the background with a restickable glue stick (see Introduction for more information), double-sided tape, or loops of tape.

Option: Wear a story apron with a number of pockets sewn to it. Tuck the figures in the pockets and take them out as you tell the story. Tell the children that when you have company, you wear an apron to protect your clothes when you are getting the food ready for your company to eat. Or, show the pictures and tell the story using the Arch Book *What's for Lunch?* (CPH, 59-1510).

Say **When Jesus lived on earth, He did many wonderful things. He taught people about His Father in heaven. He forgave their sins. He healed those who were sick. One day, Jesus went to a quiet place to rest.** Pretend to walk up an incline; then sit down. Add Jesus (4-1) to Background A. **Many people followed Jesus.** Walk in place.

Jesus saw the people coming (hold hand above eyes as if looking at crowd in the distance). **He knew they would be hungry because it was suppertime. So, Jesus asked His friends, the disciples, where they could find food to feed the people. Philip said, "We don't have enough money to buy food for everyone, Jesus. There are too many people!"** Add Philip (4-2).

But Andrew said, "Here is a little boy who has five small loaves of bread and two itty-bitty fish." Hold up two fingers; then five. Add Andrew (4-3) and boy (4-4). **"But that won't be enough for this big crowd!"**

Jesus knew what He would do. He said, "Have the people sit down." Add crowd (4-5). **Then Jesus took the bread and fish.** Add bread and fish (4-6). **He thanked His Father in heaven for the food. Then Jesus broke the bread and the fish into many pieces to give to the people. Jesus' disciple-friends passed out the bread. They passed out the fish. The people ate and ate until they weren't hungry anymore.**

Then Jesus told His disciples, "Gather up what is left." When they gathered the leftover food, there were twelve baskets full! Count to ten on your fingers; then count two more. Replace bread and fish (4-6) with leftover bread (4-7).

Jesus cared for the people and made sure they got something to eat that day. He took one small lunch and made it feed many, many people. We call what Jesus did a miracle because it is something only God can do.

Jesus cares for us and gives us what we need too! He gives us food to eat, clothes to wear, and people who love us. Best of all, Jesus died on the cross to pay for our sins. He promises to give us a wonderful home in heaven with Him.

Bible Story Review

What you do: Copy, color, and cut out Activity Page 4B. Put the paper cutouts of the two fish and five loaves of bread inside a picnic basket or lunch bag.

Key Point

In His love, God promises to care for all our physical and spiritual needs and gives us the greatest treasure: His Son and the gifts of forgiveness, life, and salvation.

Hand out the Lesson Leaflet 4, stickers, and crayons to each child. Give children stickers of fish and bread for the activity on the back of the leaflet. Use the questions to review the story, pointing to the art on the front of the leaflet. If you do the active review, video-record the children acting out the story on your tablet device. Send it home to parents this week to watch, along with a note about your collection of nonperishable goods (see "Live It Out").

Ask **What is Jesus doing?** He is telling God thank You for the food before giving it to the people to eat.

Where did Jesus get the food? The little boy brought it in his lunch.

How was Jesus able to feed so many people with just a few fish and loaves of bread? He is God. He did a miracle.

Say **God loves every person in the whole world! He cares about us and gives us the things we need. He** *provides* **for us. He gives us clothes and food and people who love us. We just heard how Jesus provided for lots of hungry people who had no food. Let's pretend we're the people in the story.** Take out the lunch bag or child's picnic basket with the paper fish and bread inside.

One day, Jesus walked to a quiet place to rest. Walk, walk, walk. Have the children walk in place like you. **Lots of people followed Him. Walk, walk, walk.** Have the children walk in place like you. **Jesus sat down and so did the people.** Have everyone sit down. **Everyone was hungry!** Rub your stomach. **A little boy said, "I have fish and bread. I'll give you some."** Take out the paper fish and bread from basket.

Jesus blessed the food and had His disciple-friends pass it out to the people. Tear little pieces of paper off of the fish and bread, and give some to each child. **Jesus did something special that day. He did something other people can't do. He took a little lunch and made enough food to feed everyone. We call what Jesus did a miracle!** Clap and shout "Hooray!" **A miracle is something only God can do. Jesus showed that He was God when He fed everyone with just a little food. No one else could do that. Jesus cares for all of us. He gives us what we need.**

Hand out leaflets and stickers. Follow the leaflet directions to do the activities. Give children the stickers of the fish and bread to add to the basket on side 2.

Bible Words

What you do: Read the Bible Words from Philippians 4:19 in the Bible so the children make the association that these words are God's words to us.

Say **The Bible says, "God will supply every need." Today, you heard how Jesus showed He is God. He cared for the people. He made enough food for all of them to eat. Jesus cares for you too.**

Ask **What are some of the things Jesus gives you?** Let children name things.

Say **Jesus gives you food and many other good gifts to enjoy. He gives you everything you need to live. Let's pass around our fish and say our Bible Words together: "God will supply every need."**

Have the children pass a paper fish from one child to the next. As they do this, say one of the words in the Bible verse each time the fish is passed from one child to the next. Repeat the verse so each child has a turn getting a fish.

③ We Live (15 minutes)

Help children grow in their understanding of what the Bible story means for their lives. Choose the activities that work best with your class.

Growing through God's Word

What you do: Cut apart the pictures on Poster B, and mount them individually on pieces of paper. Put the pictures facedown in your lap. Give several clues for each picture until the children guess what it is. Then show them the picture, and give clues for the next one. Save the pictures of Jesus with the children and the pastor holding a Bible by the baptismal font to talk about at the end.

Say **I have some pictures of things God gives us. Let's play a guessing game with them. I will give you a clue, and you guess what I'm thinking of. Are you ready? I'm thinking of something that is black and white and wags its tail when I come home.** If the children don't say "dog" right away, give another clue. When they name the item, show them the picture of the dog and give a clue for the next picture:

I'm thinking of one of my favorite things to eat. Can you guess what it is? Show picture of food. Continue in the same way with the remaining pictures. Save the pictures of Jesus and of the pastor with the Bible by the baptismal font till the end.

Wow! God sure gives us a lot of things! God gives us food. Show picture again. **He gives us clothes to wear.** Show picture of clothing. **He gives us our home.** Show picture of house. **He gives us parents and others who love and care for us.** Show picture of parents. **He gives us things to read and play with.** Show picture of toys. **He gives us friends and pets.** Show picture of children with dog. **He gives us doctors and medicine to help us get better when we are sick.** Show medicine.

In the Lord's Prayer, we pray, "Give us this day our daily bread." Does God just give us bread? No. God gives us all our food. He gives us all these other good things too. Line up pictures on the chalk ledge or tape them to the whiteboard.

God gives us even more than this! He loves us so much that He sent Jesus to be our Savior. Show picture of pastor, and point to baptismal font. **He gives us faith in Jesus and makes us His children in Baptism.** Point to Bible in the pastor's hand. **He talks to us through His Word, the Bible, and tells us that He forgives us for Jesus' sake.** Show picture of Jesus with children. **He promises to give us life with Him forever in heaven some-day. That makes me happy! Let's sing a song to say thank You to God.**

Sing the first three stanzas of "God Is So Good" (*LOSP*, p. 57). Make up new stanzas that describe the pictures from the guessing game, or invite the children to name things they are thankful for. For example:

Sing **God gives me [ice cream], God gives me [ice cream], God gives me [ice cream], He's so good to me.**
End with singing stanza 4, **I praise His name, . . .**

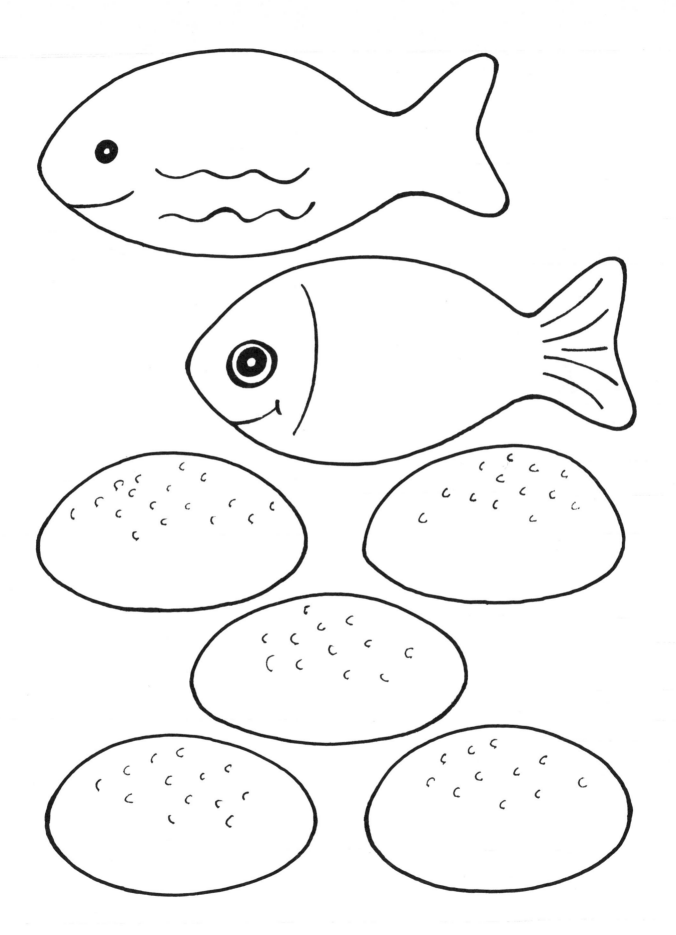

Activity Page 4B Growing in Christ® Early Childhood © 2007 Concordia Publishing House. Reproduced by permission. This page is available on the Teacher CD.

Activity Page 4C Growing in Christ® Early Childhood © 2007 Concordia Publishing House. Reproduced by permission. This page is available on the Teacher CD.

Preparing the Lesson

The Transfiguration

Matthew 17:1–9

Key Point

At the transfiguration, Jesus' glory was unveiled before the disciples. Today, His glory is unveiled for us in the Word, in the water of Baptism, and in the bread and wine of His Holy Supper. In heaven, we shall see Him in all His glory!

Law/Gospel

As a sinner, I tremble at the sound of God's voice, for I deserve punishment and am unworthy to see Him face-to-face. **As God's child, I have nothing to fear, for in His Word and Sacraments, Jesus gives me pardon and peace through His death and resurrection, making me worthy to stand face-to-face with God my Father.**

Context

Jesus' Galilean ministry is quickly drawing to a close. Soon, He will set His face toward Jerusalem and the cross. Jesus leads the inner circle of His disciples—Peter, James, and John—up a high mountain. Tradition locates the transfiguration on Mount Hermon, just north of Caesarea Philippi in Galilee. While praying, Jesus is transfigured before them and is joined by Moses and Elijah. Six days earlier, Peter had confessed Jesus to be "the Christ, the Son of the living God" (Matthew 16:16), but then rebuked Jesus when He spoke of His Passion. Peter wanted the Christ without the cross, salvation without suffering, glory without Golgotha. Moses, Elijah, and God the Father, however, confirm Jesus' words foretelling His Passion.

Commentary

In the Nicene Creed, we confess that Jesus is both true God, begotten of the Father from eternity, and true man, born of the Virgin Mary. In the transfiguration, Jesus reveals His divine glory hidden under the veil of His human flesh, and God the Father declares Him to be His beloved Son.

The children of Israel were afraid they would die if God spoke to them directly, so they pleaded with Moses to speak to them for God (Exodus 20:18–19). Scripture records that God spoke to His people through men such as Moses and Elijah—His prophets. God spoke with Moses from the burning bush on Mount Horeb (Sinai). Later, God spoke with Moses from the thick, smoky cloud covering Mount Sinai and gave him the Ten Commandments. God spoke with Elijah on Mount Horeb in a low whisper—not in the strong wind, the earthquake, or the fire. God promised to send Elijah as His messenger to prepare His way before Him.

On the Mount of Transfiguration near Jerusalem, Jesus spoke with Moses and Elijah about His departure (literally, "way out" or "exodus"; Luke 9:31). Moses and Elijah represent the Law and the Prophets (the Old Testament), which foretell Jesus' death and resurrection—our "way out" of death to life. God the Father confirmed Peter's confession and Jesus' Passion prediction; Jesus is His beloved Son, and we must "listen to Him" (Matthew 17:5).

Today, Jesus speaks to us in Scripture; we hear His sweet words especially as spoken by the pastor in the words of Absolution and in the sermon, where He veils His divine glory under the pastor's voice. As servants of the Word, pastors speak in the stead and by the command of Jesus. Jesus sprinkles us with His sin-cleansing blood veiled under the water of Holy Baptism. Jesus feeds us with His glorified body and blood veiled in, with, and under the bread and wine in the Lord's Supper. At the resurrection on the Last Day, we will see face-to-face all His heavenly glory, and we will live forever!

To hear an in-depth discussion of this Bible account, visit cph.org/podcast and listen to our Seeds of Faith podcast each week.

Lesson 5
The Transfiguration
Matthew 17:1–9

Connections

Bible Words
God sent His only Son into the world, so that we might live through Him. 1 John 4:9 (CD 6)

Faith Word
Glory

Hymn
How Sweet the Name of Jesus Sounds (*LSB* 524; CD 2)

Catechism
Apostles' Creed: Second Article

Liturgy
The Gloria Patri

Take-Home Point
Jesus is my Savior and King.

1 Opening (15 minutes)

Welcome Time

What you do: Before class, set up two activity areas. In one, put out copies of Activity Page 5A and crayons. Make copies of Activity Page Fun (below and on CD) for parents or classroom helpers. Adjust talk as necessary.

In the other activity area, put blankets or large pillows on the floor to make a mountain for the children to climb over, or set out glitter play dough.

Play the CD from your Teacher Tools to familiarize the children with the hymns and songs. In time, some will even start to hum or sing along. As the children arrive, greet each one. Give them a sticker to put on the attendance chart.

Say   Hi, [Laila], I wonder . . . do you like surprises? Today, we're going to talk about a time some of Jesus' friends got a big surprise.

Activity Page Fun Get a copy of Activity Page 5A and crayons. Show the page to your child. Have your child only color the crosses. When your child is done, talk about what he or she sees.

Say   This page has a hidden picture on it. Let's color just the sections with crosses to see what the picture is about. Do so. When your child is done coloring, continue.

Ask   Who is this? (Jesus) Today, you will hear about a time Jesus let His disciples see that He is God. Listen to find out how He looked. You can tell me about it after Sunday School.

© 2016 Concordia Publishing House. Reproduced by permission. Available on the Teacher CD.

MATERIALS NEEDED

1 Opening	2 God Speaks	3 We Live	4 Closing
Teacher Tools Attendance chart & CD	**Teacher Tools** Storytelling Figures 5-1 to 5-6 Background A Poster C CD	**Teacher Tools** Poster C	**Teacher Tools** CD
Student Pack Attendance stickers	**Student Pack** Lesson Leaflet 5 Stickers	**Student Pack** Craft Page 5 Stickers	**Student Pack** Take-home items
Other Supplies Activity Page 5A (TG) Blankets or pillows Play dough with glitter (optional) Resource Page 1 (TG, optional)	**Other Supplies** Flashlight *Jesus Shows His Glory* Arch Book (optional)	**Other Supplies** Paper or toy crown Sugar cookies or popcorn & popper Activity Page 5B (TG, optional) Paper Plus supplies (optional)	

Active Learning Encourage the children to pretend they are climbing up a mountain as they crawl or walk over the pillows or blankets. Tell them that in our story today, Jesus and His disciples go up a mountain. If you don't have the items or room to make a mountain, ask the children to pretend they are climbing a mountain with you.

Option: Purchase glitter play dough, or mix nonmetallic glitter into neon play dough. Encourage the children to make mountains and people out of the play dough. Tell them that in today's Bible story, they will hear how Jesus went up a mountain and shone with God's glory.

Use your classroom signal when it is time to clean up, or sing a cleanup song. Cue the children to join you for the opening and story.

Sing   Come and listen to God's Word, to God's Word, to God's Word. Come and listen to God's Word, from His book, the Bible.

Gathering in God's Name

What you do: Begin with this opening. To teach about the Church Year, use the materials in the Church Year Worship Kit (see the introduction for more information).

Sing   "We Are in God's House Today" (*LOSP*, p. 12; CD 15) or "The King of Glory" (*LOSP*, p. 77)

Invite the children to say the Invocation and Amen with you. Tell them "Amen" is the special word they get to say at the end of prayers, hymns, and others parts of the church service.

Begin   In the name of the Father and of the Son and of the Holy Spirit. Amen.

Offering   Have a child bring the offering basket forward. Sing an offering song.

Pray   Dear Jesus, we know that You are God. Thank You for coming to earth to be our Savior. Help us listen and learn more about Your love for us. Amen.

Celebrate   Birthdays, Baptism birthdays, and special occasions

Liturgy Link

The Gloria Patri, which means "glory to the Father," is a hymn of praise that is often sung after the Psalm or opening hymn in the Service of the Word. Read the words to the children (*LSB* 186). Tell them that today they will hear about a time Jesus showed His glory as God's Son.

2 God Speaks (20 minutes)

Story Clue

What you do: Use a flashlight. Darken the room, if possible.

Ask   What is this? Show flashlight. **Yes, it's a flashlight. What do we use a flashlight for?** Accept answers, such as, a flashlight helps us see when it's dark outside or when we need more light to find something.

Say   Our Bible story doesn't have a flashlight in it, but it tells about a time when Jesus' disciples got to see Him shine with God's glory and brightness!

Bible Story Time

What you do: Use Background A and Storytelling Figures 5-1 to 5-6. Put the figures in your Bible, and remind the children that this is a true story from

God's Word. Use a restickable glue stick (see Introduction for more information), double-sided tape, or loops of tape to attach the figures.

Option: Show the pictures and tell the story using the Arch Book *Jesus Shows His Glory* (CPH, 59-2215).

Say **God's Word tells us this true story about God's Son, Jesus. One day, Jesus took three of His disciple friends—Peter, James, and John—up a mountain to pray.** Place Jesus (5-1) and disciples (5-2) on Background A. **While Jesus was praying, a wonderful thing happened. Jesus' face became as bright as the sun, and His clothes got brighter and brighter until they were whiter than dazzling snow!** Replace Jesus (5-1) with glorified Jesus (5-3). **Jesus was showing how He looked as God's Son.**

Then something else happened to surprise the disciples. Moses (MOE zez) and Elijah (ee LIE juh) suddenly stood by Jesus. Add Moses (5-4) and Elijah (5-5). **These two men had lived on earth a long time ago. Now, God had sent them from heaven to talk to Jesus. They talked about how Jesus would soon suffer and die on the cross to pay for our sins.**

Suddenly, a big cloud came and covered everyone. Cover figures with cloud (5-6). **Then the disciples heard God say, "This is My Son, whom I love. I am happy with Him. Listen to Him."**

When the disciples heard God speaking, they were afraid. They fell down and covered their faces. Place disciples (5-2) facedown.

But Jesus came over and touched them. He told them not to be afraid, but to get up. Remove cloud, Moses, and Elijah. Replace glorified Jesus (5-3) with the other Jesus figure (5-1), and stand disciples (5-2) upright again. **When the disciples looked up, Jesus looked like He did before. After that, Jesus and the disciples went back down the mountain.**

That day, God let Peter, James, and John know in a special way that Jesus was the Savior God promised to send. They saw Jesus shining with God's glory. Now they knew that Jesus was God's Son. He had come to save them from their sins.

Someday, when we go to heaven, we will see Jesus in all His glory too. God's Son, Jesus, is our Savior and King.

Bible Story Review

What you do: Show Lesson Leaflet 5. Check for understanding by asking the questions. Then give the children Lesson Leaflet 5, stickers, and crayons or markers. For the optional activity, bring popcorn and a popcorn popper.

Ask **Who is with Jesus?** Moses and Elijah are with Jesus.

What happens to Jesus' clothes? Jesus starts to shine with God's glory, and His clothes become dazzling white.

Whose voice do they hear? God the Father speaks from the cloud.

What does God say? This is My Son, whom I love. Listen to Him.

Then direct the children's attention to the sidebar pictures on their leaflets. Have them count and find Jesus and the others in the Bible art. Give them the matching sticker for Jesus' face. Have the children trace the cloud on the front as you talk about what God said from the cloud.

On side 2, have children trace the Bible. Talk about where God speaks to

Key Point

At the transfiguration, Jesus' glory was unveiled before the disciples. Today, His glory is unveiled for us in the Word, in the water of Baptism, and in the bread and wine of His Holy Supper. In heaven, we shall see Him in all His glory.

Growing in CHRIST

us (in the Bible and in the Sacraments where He calls us to be His children and gives us His forgiveness). Have children color the Bible Words pictures, draw themselves in the circle, and add a sticker of Jesus to the cross. Talk about how God's Son, Jesus, came to be our Savior. He gives us life with Him forever.

Option: Young children benefit from both hearing the story and participating in it in some way to reinforce learning. Act out the story with the children. Assign parts of Jesus, Elijah, and Moses. Have all the remaining children pretend to be the disciples. Give them simple props if you wish, such as a Bible for Moses and a yardstick to act as a staff for Elijah.

Pretend to walk up a mountain, and kneel to pray. Darken the room and shine a flashlight on the child playing Jesus when He shines with God's glory (but do not shine the light in the child's face). Have the children playing the disciples lie down with their faces to the ground. You can speak God's words from heaven. Then have children walk back down the mountain. Discuss.

Bible Words

What you do: Read the Bible Words from 1 John 4:9 in the Bible. Play the Bible Words song on track 6 of the CD, or use the action poem to help the children learn the words. Point to Jesus on side 2 of Poster C as you introduce the verse.

Ask Who is this? Yes, Jesus! Today, you heard how Jesus shone brightly with God's glory. God the Father said Jesus is His Son and that we should listen to Him. Where do we hear Jesus speaking to us? (In His Word, the Bible)

Say The Bible tells us: "God sent His only Son into the world, so that we might live through Him." God's Son, Jesus, is our Savior and King. When we say Jesus is our Savior, it means that God forgives the wrong things we think and say and do because Jesus died for us and rose again. He is our King because He rules with His almighty power over all things and protects those who believe in Him. Someday, we will live with Jesus in a beautiful place called heaven. Let's listen to our Bible Words and then say them together. Play track 6 on the CD, and sing or say the words.

Option: Ask the children to do the actions and say the Bible Words with you.

Say		
God sent	*Point up.*	
His only Son	*Rock baby in arms.*	
into the world,	*Make a big circle with arms.*	
so that we	*Point to others, then self.*	
might live	*Walk in place.*	
through Him.	*Make a cross with fingers.*	

##

③ We Live (15 minutes)

Help children grow in their understanding of what the Bible story means for their lives. Choose the activities that work best with your class.

Growing through God's Word

What you do: Use Poster C to briefly summarize the Second Article of the Creed. Cover the pictures ahead of time with pieces of paper and remove them as you discuss each scene. To begin, hold up a paper or toy crown, or use a tablet device or smartphone to show pictures of crowns to the children.

Ask **Do you know who wears a crown?** Give the children time to answer. **Yes, a king wears a crown. A king is a person who rules over the people in his kingdom. In some places in the world, there are still kings and queens who rule over the people in their country.**

We have a King too. Who is our King? Our King is Jesus! Jesus is God's Son. Jesus rules over all things. But Jesus left the beauty and wonder of heaven to come to earth to be our Savior. Show first picture. **Jesus taught about God's love. He kept God's Law for you. Then He suffered and died on the cross because He loves you so much. He paid for your sins.** Show pictures 2 and 3. **His friends buried Him.** Show picture 4. **But Jesus didn't stay dead. He rose again on Easter.** Show picture 5. **He showed Himself to many people. Then He went back to His home in heaven.** Show picture 6. **Because you believe in Jesus, you are part of His kingdom of believers. Everyone who believes in Jesus is part of His kingdom. Most of the time while Jesus was on earth, He didn't show His glory as God's Son. But in today's Bible story, Jesus' disciples saw Him shining with God's glory.**

God gives us His Word, the Bible, so that we will know that Jesus is our Savior. We see and hear about Jesus in His Word. One day, we will see our King Jesus shining in glory with our eyes. We will see Him in all His glory in heaven. Show picture 7. **He will come again to take us to heaven to live with Him there.** Show picture 8. **Let's sing a song about our King.**

Sing "The King of Glory" (*LOSP*, p. 77) with an additional stanza.

**The King of Glory comes, the whole world rejoices;
Open the gates before Him, lift up your voices.**

**Jesus, the King of Glory, came down from heaven.
He died upon the cross, and we are forgiven.**

**The King of Glory comes, the whole world rejoices;
Open the gates before Him, lift up your voices.**

Craft Time

What you do: You will need Craft Page 5, stickers, and crayons.

Let the children color and add stickers to their crowns. Cut out the crown pieces. Tape one of the strips to each side of the crown. Then tape or staple the band sides together, adjusting band length to each child's head.

Tell the children that when we pray in the Lord's Prayer for God's kingdom to come, we are asking God to help us listen to His Word, live as His children, and help spread His kingdom by telling others about Jesus, who is our Savior and King.

Paper Plus option: Copy Activity Page 5B for each child, and give them a variety of sparkling decorating materials (e.g., sequins, glitter pens and glue, snippets of sparkling tissue paper and tinfoil). Have the children use the decorating supplies to make Jesus shine with God's glory. Talk about how Jesus shone with God's glory. Help older children draw an outline of a Bible around Jesus. Talk about how God's Word shows us Jesus and tells us He is our Savior.

Snack Time

Serve sugar cookies. Have children observe how the sugar sparkles, and talk about how Jesus shone with God's glory. *Option:* Pop popcorn, or bring kernels and popped popcorn. Show the children the kernels of corn first. Then pop the kernels, or show them the finished popcorn. Talk about how the popcorn's appearance changed.

Say **The popcorn changed from hard kernels to fluffy white popcorn! How did Jesus' face and clothes change? His clothes got whiter than popcorn, didn't they? He shone with God's glory. What did this show?** (Jesus was showing He is God's Son.)

Live It Out

Collect coins to buy supplies needed to repair used Bibles or to donate to a Bible society to purchase Bibles to send to those who do not have them. Talk about how we see and learn about Jesus in God's Word.

4 Closing (5 minutes)

Going Home

What you do: Send take-home pages and crafts home with the children. Use your CD player and CD to play the hymn.

Sing "The King of Glory" (*LOSP*, p. 77), "The Best Book of All" (*LOSP*, p. 49), or "How Sweet the Name of Jesus Sounds" (*LSB* 524; CD 2)

Say **Today, we heard how God spoke from heaven and said Jesus is His Son. Jesus shone with God's glory. He is our heavenly King who came to save us from our sins. Let's say, "Jesus is my Savior and King" together.** Say this with the children.

We can't see Jesus the way His disciples did. Instead, we see and hear Jesus speak to us in God's Word. We see just a glimpse of Jesus' glory. In God's Word, we see Jesus as God's Son and the Savior of all people. But someday, we will see Jesus in all His kingly glory when we go to heaven.

Pray **Dear Jesus, we know that You are God. Thank You for coming to earth to be our Savior. We are glad we will see You in all Your glory as our King in heaven. In Your name we pray. Amen.**

Reflection

What types of activities make it easier for your children to pay attention to the Bible story? How can you increase participation?

Pray for the Holy Spirit's guidance as you prepare lessons, asking Him to help you present the Gospel clearly so that each child will grow in faith.

Glory Be to Jesus!

Directions: Color only the sections with a cross.

Activity Page 5A Growing in Christ® Early Childhood © 2007 Concordia Publishing House. Reproduced by permission. This page is available on the Teacher CD.

Activity Page 5B Growing in Christ® Early Childhood © 2004 Concordia Publishing House. Reproduced by permission. This page is available on the Teacher CD.

Preparing the Lesson

Jesus Sends the Seventy-Two

Luke 10:1–24

Key Point

God chose the seventy-two to serve Him for a special task. God places us in various callings, giving us opportunities to serve Him and share our faith with others.

Law/Gospel

I sin when I see my calling, or vocation, as unrelated to my Lord and my faith. **God, in His mercy, uses all vocations to meet the needs of the world. In His Son, Jesus, He provides for my spiritual needs through pastors, Christian parents, and others, and He equips me to share His love with others.**

Context

Jesus sent out the Twelve (Luke 9:1–6) to proclaim the kingdom of God. Afterward, Peter confessed Jesus as the Christ (Luke 9:18–20), Jesus predicted His own death and resurrection (Luke 9:21–27), and then Jesus was transfigured (Luke 9:28–36).

When Jesus "set His face to go to Jerusalem" (Luke 9:51), He taught His disciples about the cost of following Him (Luke 9:57–62). Then He sent out the seventy-two to proclaim the kingdom of God.

Commentary

Jesus sends out seventy-two men (some manuscripts round the number off to seventy) in pairs to proclaim His kingdom and thus prepare for His upcoming visit. Jesus gives these messengers "the agenda" for their mission work: "Heal the sick in it [the town] and say to them, 'The kingdom of God has come near to you'" (Luke 10:9).

Even if some would reject them and their preaching, the seventy-two were to remain faithful to their message and know that the kingdom of God still comes, even in judgment. Jesus then lists several cities that can expect judgment because they rejected Him and His works of salvation.

Jesus uses the judgment on those cities that rejected Him and His salvation to comfort and strengthen His messengers. When they proclaim His message, He is very much present to redeem a lost and dying world. Whoever hears Jesus' messengers hears and receives Jesus Himself! When Jesus' messengers proclaim that "the kingdom of God has come near," Jesus Himself actually comes near to heal and to save.

When the seventy-two return, Jesus directs their attention away from the visible success of their work and onto the heavenly salvation He gives them. Jesus does not want His messengers to focus on earthly achievements but rather on His gifts of heavenly grace and salvation.

Jesus does not want His messengers to rejoice in their accomplishments, even if those include casting out demons. Rather, He wants them to rejoice that their names are written in God's Book of Life, along with Adam and Eve, Noah, Abraham and Sarah, Moses, David, all of the prophets, and all faithful believers through the ages.

God's favor in electing and saving us sinners is far beyond our human understanding, and yet a little child can receive it and trust it. We may not be able to mentally grasp the inner workings of the triune God ("All things have been handed over to Me by My Father" [Luke 10:22]), but we can take comfort in knowing that the Father reveals His favor and mercy through His Son, Jesus. In turn, Jesus reveals God's favor and mercy through the messengers and ministry of His Church.

To hear an in-depth discussion of this Bible account, visit cph.org/podcast and listen to our Seeds of Faith podcast each week.

Lesson 6

Jesus Sends the Seventy-Two

Luke 10:1–24

Connections

Bible Words
[Jesus says,] "Tell . . . how much the Lord has done for you." Mark 5:19

Faith Word
Gospel, Good News

Hymn
I Am Jesus' Little Lamb (*LSB* 740; CD 3)

Catechism
Apostles' Creed:
Third Article (CD 16)

Take-Home Point
God helps me share His love and tell about Jesus.

1 Opening (15 minutes)

Welcome Time

What you do: Before class, set up two activity areas. In one, put out copies of Activity Page 6, hat stickers from the Sticker Page, and crayons. Make copies of Activity Page Fun (below and on CD) for parents or classroom helpers. Adjust talk as necessary.

In the other activity area, set out toy people figures, or plan to take the children on a field trip to church.

Play the CD from your Teacher Tools to familiarize the children with the hymns and songs. In time, some will even start to hum or sing along. As the children arrive, greet each one. Give each a sticker to put on the attendance chart.

Say Hi, [Sebastian], what did you do this week? Where did you go? Build relationships with the children by actively listening; then get them started in one of the learning areas to build interest and readiness for the lesson.

Activity Page Fun Get a copy of Activity Page 6 and a set of hat stickers. Show the page to your child, pointing to each person on it, one at a time.

Ask What do you think this person does? God makes each of us special and gives us work to do. Give your child hat stickers to match to the people on the page, and have your child color the people. Today, you will hear how Jesus chose some helpers and gave them the job of telling others about God's love.

© 2016 Concordia Publishing House. Reproduced by permission. Available on the Teacher CD.

MATERIALS NEEDED

1 Opening	2 God Speaks	3 We Live	4 Closing
Teacher Tools Attendance chart & CD	**Teacher Tools** Poster C Poster D	**Student Pack** Craft Page 6 Stickers	**Teacher Tools** CD
Student Pack Attendance stickers Activity Page stickers	**Student Pack** Lesson Leaflet 6 Stickers	**Other Supplies** Occupational items in bag Sprout	**Student Pack** Take-home materials
Other Supplies Activity Page 6 (TG) Toy people figures Resource Page 1 (TG, optional)	**Other Supplies** Colored paper Heart & cross cookie cutter or online patterns	Heavy paper or note cards Trail mix & paper lunch bags O-shaped cereal or sandpaper (optional) Paper Plus supplies (optional)	

Active Learning Set out toy people figures.

Ask **Where are the people going? Whom will they meet? In today's Bible story, Jesus tells some helpers to go to lots of places and tell others about God's love. What can these helpers say about Jesus to those they meet?** Encourage the children to role-play having the toy people say "Jesus loves you" and "Jesus died for you."

Option: Visit the church. Point out where the pastor stands when he reads God's Word (the lectern). Show the children the Bible. Ask them to show you where the pastor stands to teach them about God's love (the pulpit).

Ask **What does Pastor do at the altar?** (He prays; he speaks God's Word; he tells us our sins are forgiven for Jesus' sake; etc.) **What happens at the baptismal font?** Discuss. Tell children they will hear how Jesus sent special helpers to tell about Him. **Who are the special helpers at church who tell you about Jesus?** (The pastor, deaconess, Sunday School teachers, etc.)

Use your classroom signal when it is time to clean up. Sing a cleanup song (Resource Page 1). Cue the children to join you for the opening and story.

Sing **Come and listen to God's Word, to God's Word, to God's Word. Come and listen to God's Word, from His book, the Bible.**

Gathering in God's Name

What you do: Begin with this opening. To teach about the Church Year, use the materials in the Church Year Worship Kit (see introduction).

Sing "We Are in God's House Today" (*LOSP*, p. 12; CD 15) or "This Little Gospel Light of Mine" (*LOSP*, p. 103)

Invite the children to say the Invocation and Amen with you. Tell them "Amen" is the special word they get to say at the end of prayers, hymns, and others parts of the church service.

Begin **In the name of the Father and of the Son and of the Holy Spirit. Amen.**

Offering Have a child bring the offering basket forward. Sing an offering song.

Pray **Dear Jesus, thank You for giving us pastors and teachers to tell us of Your love. Help us to listen and learn about You. Amen.**

Celebrate Birthdays, Baptism birthdays, and special occasions

2 God Speaks (20 minutes)

Story Clue

What you do: You will need Poster C with the figure of Jesus and cookie cutters in the shape of a heart and a cross, or find online patterns of a heart and cross. Lightly trace around the heart onto a piece of red paper and around the cross onto a piece of brown paper or sandpaper. You will also need a pair of scissors for cutting the heart and cross from the papers. Begin by holding up the red paper in a way so children don't see the heart on it.

Ask **What does red remind you of?** Accept responses. Cut out and hold up the heart. **Red makes me think of hearts, and hearts remind me of love. Who loves you?** Accept responses. **Our moms and dads and friends and others love us. But most of all, Jesus loves us.** Hold up the brown paper.

What does the color brown remind you of? Listen to responses. **This is what brown makes me think of.** Cut out the cross, and show it to the children. **Jesus loved us so much that He died on the cross to pay for all our sins—the wrong things we think and say and do. But Jesus didn't stay dead, did He?** Point to Jesus on side 2 of Poster C. **On Easter, Jesus became alive again. He promises that someday, everyone who believes in Him will live with Him in heaven.**

These three things tell a story. Hold up the heart: **Jesus loves us.** Hold up the cross: **Jesus died for us.** Hold up the Jesus poster: **Jesus is alive and promises to be with us always. Someday, we will live with Him in heaven. Isn't that Good News? We call this Good News the Gospel. Jesus wants everyone to know this Good News! In our Bible story today, Jesus sends out special helpers to tell people this Good News.**

Bible Story Time

What you do: Use Poster D.

Say **The Bible tells us that Jesus came to do special work on earth. He came to be our Savior from sin. Jesus wanted people to know about God's love. He wanted them to know that God had sent Him to be their Savior. So one day, Jesus chose seventy-two special helpers.** Show picture and count the helpers shown on it: 1, 2, 3, . . . When you run out, say: **Wow! There isn't enough room on this picture to show all the helpers Jesus sent out. There were many more than this!**

Jesus told these helpers, "I have a special job for you to do. I want you to go to the villages and towns and cities. Tell the people about God's love. Heal the sick people. I want everyone to hear and believe that I am the Savior God promised to send."

So the seventy-two helpers did just what Jesus told them to do. Two of them went down a road to one village. Hold up two fingers; make them "walk." **Two others went to a city.** Hold up two fingers; make them "walk" in a different direction. **Two went to another town.** Hold up two fingers; "walk" them a different way. **Soon all the helpers were walking from place to place.** Make fingers "walk" again. **Everywhere they went, they healed sick people. Everywhere they went, they told people about God's love.**

When they came back, they were so happy. They told Jesus, "We told people the Good News of God's love. We told them God was keeping His promise to send the Savior. We healed sick people in Your name." Point to Poster D again.

Jesus was happy to hear what they said. "I'm glad," He said, "and so is God. You are part of His family and so are many others now." After that, Jesus thanked His heavenly Father for being with His helpers. Jesus was happy they had told many people the Good News that He had come to be the Savior.

Jesus gave these helpers special work to do. Jesus gives us pastors and deaconesses and missionaries and teachers to tell others the Good News that Jesus is our Savior. Because we are God's children, we can

Key Point

God chose the seventy-two to serve Him for a special task. God places us in various callings, giving us opportunities to serve Him and share our faith with others.

show His love for others and tell them about Jesus too. We can invite them to come to church and Sunday School with us. Jesus wants everyone to hear that He is the Savior God promised to send.

Bible Story Review

What you do: Show the picture on Poster D, and review the story with the review questions. Then hand out Lesson Leaflet 6, stickers, and crayons.

Ask **Where is Jesus sending the special helpers?** To villages and towns and cities

What does He want them to do? Tell everyone they meet about Him and how God sent Him to be the Savior of the world

Who tells you about Jesus? Let children tell.

Whom can you tell about Jesus? Let children tell.

On their leaflets, have the children look for the helpers Jesus sent out and the picture of Jesus in the Bible story art. Match the stickers to the pictures. On side 2, ask children to point to those who need to hear about Jesus. Tell them to color the pictures of those who are helping others learn of Him.

Option: Use the heart, the cross, and the Jesus picture again.

Say Show heart. **We know Jesus loves us.** Show cross. **We know He paid for our sins on the cross.** Show Jesus picture. **We know He came alive again and is with us always. Jesus wants *everyone* to know that He loves them and died for them. He uses His people to tell this Good News.**

Jesus sent special helpers to tell others. Our pastors tell us about Jesus too. But Jesus uses all of us to share His love and tell others. What are some things you can tell about Jesus? Accept answers.

Bible Words

What you do: Read Mark 5:19 from the Bible. Use the activity to reinforce the words.

Say In the Bible, [Jesus says,] "Tell . . . how much the Lord has done for you." Jesus chose special helpers and sent them to tell others about Him. Jesus gives us pastors and teachers and parents and others to tell us about His love. He makes you helpers too. You can show His love and tell others about Him. Let's say our Bible Words together. *Lead the children in saying the words and doing the actions.*

Say **Tell . . .**   *Cup hands around mouth.*
how much   *Hold hands out wide.*
the Lord   *Point up.*
has done   *Make two fists; hit them alternately on each other.*
for you.   *Point to several children.*

③ We Live (15 minutes)

Help children grow in their understanding of what the Bible story means for their lives. Choose the activities that work best with your class.

Growing through God's Word

What you do: Put a Bible and several items representing different occupations inside a tote bag (e.g., a tool, a mixing bowl and whisk, a play medical kit). Have Sprout carry the bag in.

Teacher: Hi, Sprout! (*Sprout rummages in the bag.*) What are you doing?

Sprout: I'm trying to decide what I want to be when I grow up. I thought I might get some good ideas if I looked in my dress-up bag. (*Pulling out a tool*) Maybe I could be a construction worker. (*Pulling out the medical kit*) Or I could be a doctor or nurse. (*Continue in same manner with a few more items.*)

Teacher: Oh, Sprout, you have a long time before you're all grown up and have to get a job. You have lots of time to think about what you want to be.

Sprout: I know, but I want to do something that would make Jesus happy. (*He pulls out a Bible.*) Maybe I should be a pastor. Would that make Jesus happy?

Teacher: Jesus would be happy if you grew up to be a pastor, Sprout, but He will be happy if you want to be a farmer or a computer operator or a store worker too. You don't have to worry about what you will be. Jesus loves you and has made you His child. He is happy with you right now.

Sprout: But in our story it said there's lots of work to do. God wants everyone to know the Good News about Jesus' dying on the cross and coming back to life again. If I were a pastor, I could tell people about Jesus.

Teacher: That's true, Sprout, you could. And that would be a good thing. God gives us pastors to do the special job of teaching others about Jesus. But you can still tell people about Jesus if you're not a pastor. You can invite someone to church or Sunday School. You can share Jesus' love with others right now. You don't have to wait till you grow up.

Sprout: Oh, I never thought about that. What else can I do?

Teacher: You can pray that God would send workers to tell everyone about Jesus so all people will hear that Jesus died for their sins.

Sprout: I know how to pray!

Teacher: Sure you do, Sprout. Why don't we all pray together?

Pray **Dear Jesus, thank You for pastors and teachers. Help them tell lots of people about You! Help us to share Your love with others too, by what we say and do. Amen.**

Craft Time

What you do: You will need Craft Page 6, stickers, and crayons. *Option:* To add texture to the path, give students snippets of sandpaper or O-shaped cereal. Have the children attach the sticker of the men to a piece of paper or a note card. Fold the paper in half with the men on top. Trim to the size of the men. You will have a tent-card figure.

On side 1 of the Craft Page, have the children move their men along the path to talk to people about Jesus, to heal sick people in His name, and, finally, to return to Jesus. If you did not make tent puppets, have the children attach the sticker of the men to the page and use their pencil to draw their path. Give them sandpaper or cereal to glue to the path, if desired.

Say **Jesus sent out seventy-two helpers to show and tell others about God's love for them. He told them to tell people that He is the Savior**

Growing in CHRiST.

they had been waiting for. **Move your men (or draw a line) from where the people start to the first man and woman you see. What will they tell them about Jesus?**

Now, move them (draw a line) to the house where they will stay for the night and talk to people about Jesus. What will they say? Now move them (draw a line) to the sick people that they will make well with God's power. Now move the men (draw a line) to Jesus. What will they tell Jesus about their work?

Turn the paper over. Talk about the scenes and ways to share Jesus' love with others. Let the children finish coloring the scenes and add stickers of flowers and an offering. If you have time, play the game with the children.

Paper Plus option: Make prayer cards. Write a Bible verse that tells about God's love in Jesus or a prayer on the bottom half of a piece of paper. Copy the page for each child onto colored paper. Have children fold the page in half and decorate it with markers, stickers, and other embellishments. On the inside, they can draw a picture and sign their name.

Snack Time

Serve trail mix. Put the snack for the day in a small paper bag, rolled over like a lunch bag. Put each child's name on the bag.

Live It Out

On poster paper or your board, make two lists. First, list people who tell about Jesus (e.g., pastors, teachers, missionaries). Then list people you and the children can tell about Jesus. Have children choose someone from one of the lists to whom they can send a prayer card (Paper Plus option) to say thank you or to share Jesus' love.

4 Closing (5 minutes)

Going Home

What you do: Send home take-home pages and crafts. Cue CD.

Sing "I Can Tell" (*LOSP*, p. 99; CD 11) or "I Am Jesus' Little Lamb" (*LSB* 740; CD 3)

Say **Today, we learned that Jesus wants everyone to hear that He is the Savior of the world. He gives us pastors and missionaries to tell the Good News about Jesus. He helps us share His love and tell others too.**

Help the children say, "God helps me share His love and tell about Jesus." Then have them echo your words at each asterisk as you pray.

Pray **Dear God,* bless all pastors and teachers.* Help them* tell others about You.* Help us* to share Your love* and tell others too.* In Jesus' name we pray.* Amen.***

Reflection

Did the children begin to grasp that God uses people to tell others about Jesus? Was each child able to say something about God's love today? Think of ways you can help them do that next week.

Tell . . . how much the Lord has done for you. Mark 5:19

Activity Page 6 *Growing in Christ*® Early Childhood © 2007 Concordia Publishing House. Scripture: ESV®. Reproduced by permission. This page is available on the Teacher CD.

Preparing the Lesson

The Good Samaritan

Luke 10:25–37

Key Point

God calls us to act in love toward all people, even our enemies, but we often pass by on the other side, ignoring our neighbor in need. Jesus is the Good Samaritan to us, healing us from sin and restoring us to eternal life.

Law/**Gospel**

God's command to love my neighbor is a command to be perfectly compassionate to everyone I meet. **Though I fall short, Jesus is the Good Samaritan, who binds up my brokenness, forgives my sin, and restores me to eternal life.**

Context

Jesus is traveling from Galilee to Jerusalem, aware that this journey will end in His crucifixion (Luke 9:51). Jesus teaches, preaches, and works miracles along the way, reflecting His merciful character.

Commentary

The man was not a secular lawyer, but a teacher of the Law within the synagogue. When he puts Jesus to the test, he is trying to show that Jesus is teaching something foreign to Scripture and is therefore a false teacher. His question, "What shall I do to inherit eternal life?" is meant to trap Jesus. Jesus refers him to the very Law that the man had studied his whole life. The man knows the answer to his question: Fulfill the two greatest commandments—love God and love your neighbor—then you can go to heaven. Thinking obedience to the Law is the path to eternal life, the man attempts to narrow the requirement of "mercy toward all" to "mercy toward some" with the question, "Who is my neighbor?" (Luke 10:29).

To answer the question, Jesus tells a parable about a man who fell among thieves and was beaten, robbed, and left for dead. A temple priest and a Levite, both of whom lived by the teachings of Mosaic Law, passed by the man. Finally, a Samaritan, a foreigner from another place, stops, helps, pours on medicine, bandages the man's wounds,

and bears him to a place of healing and rest, paying for it all himself and promising to come again. Jesus concludes the parable by asking, "Who proved to be a neighbor to the man who fell among the robbers?" The answer is "the one who showed mercy." Jesus' story illustrates not only the compassion necessary in keeping these commandments but also how easily and often we fall short.

Keeping God's commandments is more than outward conformity to principles. The priest and Levite could claim that they were technically trying to keep the Law by avoiding potential uncleanness (which they would have incurred if the victim was dead or defiled in some way). The Samaritan, who technically was bound by the same laws of cleanliness, demonstrates that the heart of the Law is love and compassion. To love one's neighbor is to put that person before one's own conveniences and daily life. To love one's neighbor is to help anyone who is encountered.

Through this parable, Jesus teaches us that fulfilling the Law requires continuous love and compassion. This means all of us have fallen short in caring for our neighbors. Our best efforts to "go and do likewise" are exposed as total failures in light of God's Law. But Jesus, the true Good Samaritan, has not fallen short. He came to do everything for salvation, leaving nothing for man to earn. He found us, dying sinners totally estranged from God, and paid all He had—perfect obedience during His life and a sacrificial death for our sins—in order to redeem us. He gives medicine that heals all sins, including the sin of lacking mercy. He will bear people to a place of refuge, the church, where they can be taken care of and receive more medicine. Then Jesus promises to come back to take all believers to Himself in heaven.

To hear an in-depth discussion of this Bible account, visit cph.org/podcast and listen to our Seeds of Faith podcast each week.

The Good Samaritan

Luke 10:25–37

Connections

Bible Words

[Jesus says,] "Just as I have loved you, you also are to love one another." John 13:34

Faith Word

Neighbor

Hymn

I Am Jesus' Little Lamb (*LSB* 740; CD 3)

Catechism

Apostles' Creed: Second Article

Take-Home Point

God wants me to show love for others.

 Opening (15 minutes)

Welcome Time

What you do: Before class, set up two activity areas. In one, put out copies of Activity Page 7A and crayons. Make copies of Activity Page Fun (below and on CD) for parents or classroom helpers. Adjust talk as necessary.

In the other activity area, set out paper, markers, and heart and cross stencils. To make stencils, cut heart and cross shapes out of plastic lids from non-dairy topping containers, whipped butter or cream cheese containers, or the like. *Option:* Set out play dough and cookie cutters shaped like hearts and crosses.

Play the CD from your Teacher Tools to familiarize the children with the hymns and songs. In time, some will even start to hum or sing along. As the children arrive, greet each one. Give them a sticker to put on the attendance chart.

Say Hi, [Mia], have you ever fallen down and needed someone to help you? Who helped? Today, you'll hear a story Jesus told about a man who needed help.

Activity Page Fun Get a copy of Activity Page 7A to show your child.

Say Here is a picture of children at the park. Look for the children who are showing love. Circle them. How are they being a good friend? Let your child tell. **Today, you'll hear a story Jesus told about someone who was a good friend to someone he didn't even know.**

© 2016 Concordia Publishing House. Reproduced by permission. Available on the Teacher CD.

MATERIALS NEEDED

1 Opening	2 God Speaks	3 We Live	4 Closing
Teacher Tools Attendance chart & CD	**Teacher Tools** Poster E	**Teacher Tools** Craft Page 7 Stickers	**Teacher Tools** CD
Student Pack Attendance stickers	**Student Pack** Lesson Leaflet 7	**Other Supplies** Story bag & items Granola bars or trail mix & cups of water Activity Pages 7B & 7C (TG, optional) Shoebox (optional) Paper Plus supplies (optional)	**Student Pack** Take-home items
Other Supplies Activity Page 7A (TG) Paper & stencils of a heart & cross Play dough & heart & cross cookie cutters (optional) Resource Page 1 (TG, optional)	**Other Supplies** Soap, ointment, Band-Aids & gauze in story bag Activity Pages 7B & 7C (TG) Shoebox & cups Cookie sheet & cornmeal *The Story of the Good Samaritan* Arch Book (optional)		

Active Learning Show children how to use the stencils to make a picture. If you set out play dough, show the children how to make hearts and crosses by rolling it into ropes and shaping them into hearts and crosses or by using the cookie cutters. Adapt talk as needed.

Say **Hearts and crosses make me think of Jesus and His love. You can use the hearts and crosses to make a picture for someone who needs cheering up. Doing kind things for others shows love for them. When you share the markers and stencils, you are showing love for one another too. You are being a good friend. Today, you'll hear a story about a man who was hurt. God sent someone to be his friend and help him.**

Use your classroom signal when it is time to clean up. Sing this cleanup song to the tune of "Row, Row, Row Your Boat."

Sing **Help, help, helping hands, helping through the day,**
Showing Jesus we love Him, in, oh, so many ways.

Gathering in God's Name

What you do: Gather the children, and begin with this opening. To teach about the Church Year, use the materials in the Church Year Worship Kit.

Sing "We Are in God's House Today" (*LOSP*, p. 12; CD 15) or another song

Invite the children to say the Invocation and Amen with you. Tell them "Amen" is the special word they get to say at the end of prayers and the like.

Begin **In the name of the Father and of the Son and of the Holy Spirit. Amen.**

Offering Ask a child to bring the offering basket forward. Sing an offering song.

Pray **Dear Jesus, thank You for being our Friend and Savior. Help us to love You and other people. Help us to be good helpers. Forgive us when we do not help. Amen.**

Celebrate Birthdays, Baptism birthdays, and special occasions

2 God Speaks (20 minutes)

Story Clue

What you do: Put a bar of soap, a box of Band-Aids, some gauze, and a tube of antibiotic cream in your story bag.

Say **Hi, friends. I noticed you were good helpers today! Some of you used your hands to make a picture. When you worked together and shared the art supplies, you were showing love for one another. Today, we are going to hear a story Jesus told about being a helper and showing love. But first, I need some helpers. I put some clues about our Bible story in my story bag. Who wants to help take the clues out of the bag?**

Invite one child at a time to come take an item out of your bag. Comment on what each item is used for as it is taken out.

Ask **What is this? What is it used for?** Let children offer suggestions. (Band-Aids) **If you get a cut or scrape, you often put a Band-Aid on it.**

(Bar of soap) **We wash away dirt and germs with soap.**
(Antibiotic cream) **This is a type of medicine. If you get a big cut or burn, your mom or dad might put some of this cream on it to help it heal.**
(Gauze) **When someone gets a big cut or gash, a little Band-Aid won't cover it. So, a helper wraps the cut in gauze like this.**

Say Hmm, I wonder . . . what do these things have to do with our Bible story? I'll give you a clue. In today's Bible story, a man uses some things like this to help someone. Let's listen and find out more.

Bible Story Time

What you do: Copy Activity Pages 7B and 7C. Color and cut apart the figures. Glue them to upside-down cups to make cuppets. Put the cuppets on a cookie sheet covered with cornmeal. If you have an old shoebox, cut a door in the side of it, and turn it upside down for the inn.

Gather the children around you as you tell the story so they can see and hear. Mark your Bible text with a bookmark. Open your Bible to Luke 10:25–37. *Option:* Show Poster E or the pictures in *The Story of the Good Samaritan* Arch Book (CPH, 59-1596) as you tell the story.

Say **When Jesus lived on earth, He taught people about God's love. Many people came to listen to Him. Did you know that you and I can listen to Jesus too? He speaks to us in His Word, the Bible.** Show children your Bible. **Are you ready to listen?** Hold up the Jesus cuppet (7-1) to get the children's attention.

One day, a man came to Jesus and wanted to know what he had to do to get to heaven. The man thought, "I'm very good. I don't need God to forgive me." Jesus told the man, "You must love God with all your heart and your neighbor as yourself."

The man asked, "Who is my neighbor?" To answer him, Jesus told him a story. The story shows that no one is as good as God. We all need God's forgiveness. This is the story Jesus told (put cuppet to the side)**:**

A man walked down the road to Jericho. Put traveling man (7-2) on cookie sheet. **All of a sudden, some robbers jumped out from behind a rock. They hit the man and took all his things. Then they ran away. The man lay hurt and bleeding by the road.** Replace man with injured man (7-3).

Along came a priest who worked in the temple-church. Add priest (7-4). **He saw the hurt and bleeding man. Surely he would help him. But no, the priest just kept walking down the road.**

A second man came by who also worked in the temple-church. Add Levite (7-5). **Surely he would stop and help the hurt man. But no, he just walked by too.**

Then a man from Samaria (suh MARE ee uh) **came along.** Add Samaritan and his donkey (7-6). **Would he help the hurt man? Yes, he saw the poor, hurt man, and felt sorry for him. He knelt down to help.**

He took some oil and rubbed it on the man's wounds. He bandaged the man's sores. Then he put the man on his donkey. Replace cuppets with injured man on donkey (7-7) and Samaritan (7-8).

The Samaritan (suh MARE ih tuhn) **took the hurt man to an inn where he would be cared for.** Add shoebox, if you made one, and innkeeper (7-9).

Key Point

God calls us to act in love toward all people, even our enemies, but we often pass by on the other side, ignoring our neighbor in need. Jesus is the Good Samaritan to us, healing us from sin and restoring us to eternal life.

The Samaritan had to leave. But he gave the innkeeper some money and asked him to take care of the hurt man. Now the hurt man would have food to eat and water to drink until he was able to travel again. Set cookie sheet aside.

Say **When Jesus finished the story, He asked, "Which man showed he was loving and helping? Who was a kind neighbor?" A listener said, "The one who helped the hurting man." Jesus said, "I want you to be a kind and loving neighbor too."**

Jesus wants us to be loving neighbors, or helpers, too. He wants us to show love for others, and He helps us do this. But Jesus helps us and shows love for us in an even better way. Do you know how? Jesus came to rescue us from our sins by dying on the cross for us. Someday, He will take us to heaven where there will be no more hurts or sadness.

Bible Story Review

What you do: Show Poster E. Ask these questions to review. Then hand out Lesson Leaflet 7 and crayons.

Ask **What happened to the hurt man?** Some robbers beat him up.

How does the Samaritan man help him? He cleaned his wounds, put bandages on him, and took him to a safe place to get better.

How does Jesus help you? Jesus shows love for us in many ways, especially by saving us from our sins.

Hand out the leaflets and crayons. Have children describe what's happening in the sidebar pictures, then circle the appropriate numbers to indicate their story order. On side 2, children can use their finger then a crayon to complete the maze.

Option: Video-record the children as they act out the story, or let them manipulate the cuppets as you read or paraphrase the story on the back of the leaflet. Let them watch the video.

Bible Words

What you do: Bookmark John 13:34 in your Bible. Ask for a helper to come up and open the Bible for you at the bookmark. Thank him or her.

Say **[Gabriel] is one of our helpers today. Who is our best Helper though? Jesus! He is our Savior and Helper! Because Jesus loves us so much, we want to help others and show love for them too.** Open Bible.

In the Bible, [Jesus says,] "Just as I have loved you, you also are to love one another." Can you say that with me?

[Jesus says,]	*Point up.*
"Just as I have loved you,	*Cross hands over heart; point to others.*
you also are to love	*Point to others; cross hands over heart*
one another."	*Point to others.*

Option: Sing "We Love" (*LOSP,* p. 54)

③ We Live (15 minutes)

Help children grow in their understanding of what the Bible story means for their lives. Choose the activities that work best with your class.

Growing through God's Word

What you do: Show the Band-Aids, gauze, soap, and ointment to make a connection from the story to ways the children can help and show love for others.

Ask **Which man showed love and was a helper? Yes, the Samaritan.** Show story clues. **He cleaned the man's cuts and wrapped them in bandages. Jesus wants us to be helpers and show love for others too. Can you think of times you can be a helper either here or at home?** Accept answers. If needed, give suggestions. Then lead children in this activity.

Say **Now let's act out ways we can help. Find a friend and hold hands. Pretend one of you falls down and is hurt. How can the other friend help? Yes, the friend can show love by helping his or her partner get up. Let's sing about that. As we sing, act out helping a partner get up.** Sing to the tune of "London Bridge Is Falling Down."

Sing **I can help my friend get up, Friend get up, friend get up. I can help my friend get up. I can help.** (Sing "help" for two notes.)

Say **Let's sing about some of the other things you named.** Sing stanzas using suggestions the children gave, acting out the examples:

I can help to fold the clothes . . .	*Pretend to fold clothes.*
I can help to pick up toys . . .	*Pretend to pick up toys.*
I can help to give a hug . . .	*Hug self.*

Those are all great ways to help. Jesus helps us to show love for others. But sometimes we don't feel like helping or we forget to help. We act like the first two men in the story Jesus told. Was that a bad thing to do—not to help the hurt man? Yes, it was bad. God, our Father, is kind to everyone, and He wants us to be kind too.

When we say "I won't help," we are not being kind. We are doing a bad thing. God is not pleased with that at all. But He still loves us and sent Jesus to die for all the bad things we do, and the good things we *should* do, but don't. When we do bad things, we can ask Jesus to forgive us. Jesus forgives our sins. And He will help us to do better.

Craft Time

What you do: Hand out Craft Page 7, stickers, and markers. Point to the Search and Find activity on side 2. Then talk about the helper chart.

Say **Here is a picture of a Sunday School picnic.** Point to pictures at the top. **Can you find these things in the picture?** Give children time to do this. Then direct attention to the Bible Words and hand out those stickers.

Let's read the Bible Words and add stickers. Do so. **Jesus loves us so much that He died on the cross for us. He tells us to love one another. Look at the children in the picture. Which ones are being helpers and**

Growing in CHRIST.

showing love? A boy is helping his grandpa get to the park; a child is giving Pastor a drink; another is helping a friend who has fallen, and so forth.

Jesus helps us to do kind and loving things too. Turn to the helper chart. **Here is a chart that shows some of the ways you can help and show love for others.** Read the words under each picture. **What are some things you can do?** Let children tell. **You can take your heart stickers home and add a sticker to a picture on the chart whenever you do something this week. If you run out of stickers, draw a heart or cross.**

Sometimes we don't do kind and helpful things, though, do we? When we do bad things, we ask Jesus to forgive us and to help us do better. We can trust our Savior, Jesus, to always be our Helper and Friend.

Paper Plus option: Copy Activity Pages 7B and 7C for each child to make storytelling figures. Have children color and cut out the figures, then tape them to upside-down cups or craft sticks, which can be stuck in lumps of play dough at home. Encourage them to use the figures to tell the story to grown-ups at home. Tell them they can ask a grown-up to help them make an inn using an old shoebox. Caution them not to use scissors without permission.

Snack Time

Provide granola bars or trail mix and cups of water. Point out that the Samaritan and man probably took their own food with them on the trip because there weren't fast-food places in their day. Talk about ways the Samaritan showed love and the ways God helps us to show love for others.

Live It Out

Search lcms.org for social ministry projects your class can do, or make personal care or school kits to distribute locally to those in need or to send to a world relief agency such as Lutheran World Relief. Search online for what goes in each kit.

Faith in Action!

4 Closing (5 minutes)

Going Home

What you do: Send home take-home pages and crafts. Cue CD.

Sing "Jesus Wants Me for a Helper" (*LOSP*, p. 33) or "I Am Jesus' Little Lamb" (*LSB* 740; CD 3)

Say **God wants us to show love for others. He helps us to do this. Let's say "God wants me to show love for others" together.** Do so. **Sometimes we don't do this. Let's ask Jesus to forgive us for these times.**

Pray **Dear Jesus, we are not always nice to others. Forgive us and help us think of good things we can do for them. Thank You for loving us and saving us from the hurt of our sin by dying on the cross for us. Amen.**

Reflection

Were the children able to identify ways to be helpers and show love for others? Do they understand that they can't be perfect helpers, but that Jesus forgives them and will help them to do better? Remember God's promises to love and forgive you. He will give you strength to show love for others.

Who Is Being a Good Friend?

Circle the children who are showing love for others.

Activity Page 7A Growing in Christ® Early Childhood © 2009, 2016 Concordia Publishing House. Reproduced by permission. This page is available on the Teacher CD.

The Good Samaritan Story Figures

Activity Page 7B Growing in Christ® Early Childhood © 2004, 2016 Concordia Publishing House. Reproduced by permission. This page is available on the Teacher CD.

The Good Samaritan Story Figures

7-7

7-8

7-9

Activity Page 7C Growing in Christ® Early Childhood © 2004, 2016 Concordia Publishing House. Reproduced by permission. This page is available on the Teacher CD.

Preparing the Lesson

The Good Shepherd

John 10:1–18

Date of Use

Key Point

We are like sheep who have gone astray. Jesus is the Good Shepherd, who rescues, gathers, and cares for us through His Word and Sacraments.

Law/**Gospel**

Because of sin, I face physical and spiritual danger in this world. **Jesus, my Good Shepherd, guards and protects me from sin, death, and the power of the devil, feeding me through His Word and Sacraments to keep my faith strong.**

Context

Jesus is in Jerusalem. Earlier, He had given sight to a man born blind. In chapter 10, we see Jesus addressing the Jews gathered there, including the Pharisees and other religious leaders.

Commentary

In the Old Testament, God often compared His relationship to His people as a Shepherd to His sheep (Psalm 23; Isaiah 40:10–11; Ezekiel 34:11–16). In Ezekiel 34:23, God promised that He would place over His people one Shepherd who would tend them. In John 10, Jesus identifies Himself as that Good Shepherd. By stating that He is the Good Shepherd, Jesus asserts that He is God and one with the Father (John 10:30). As the Good Shepherd, He knows His sheep by name. He lays down His life for His sheep and gives them eternal life.

The imagery of shepherd and sheep contrasts the love and mercy of Christ with our helplessness and dependence on Him. A lost sheep cannot find its way home and will certainly become prey for wild animals. However, Jesus, our Good Shepherd, found us and rescued us when we were lost in sin and unbelief. Now, He watches over and protects us. He has come so that in place of eternal death apart from Him, we now have life and have it abundantly. As His sheep, we hear His voice and follow Him. When by our sin we wander away from Him, it is His Word of repentance and forgiveness that draws us back to Him.

Jesus identifies thieves and robbers who seek to steal the sheep. These would be false teachers, who by their lies lead people away from Christ. These false teachers included the Pharisees and religious authorities, who by their man-made rules and lack of love and concern for the welfare of the people led many people away from the faith. In Ezekiel 34:1–10, God condemned those who were false shepherds. Instead of listening to the voice of those who are thieves and robbers, the Lord's sheep listen to His voice and follow Him.

In addition to identifying Himself as the Shepherd, Jesus says that He is the door of the sheep (John 10:7, 9). Jesus not only leads us and guides us as our Shepherd, but He is also the door by which we enter to become sheep of His fold. "We are the people of His pasture, and the sheep of His hand" (Psalm 95:7). Thus, He promises: "If anyone enters by Me, he will be saved and will go in and out and find pasture" (John 10:9). We entered that gate and were made His sheep through Baptism, and He continues to lead us out to green pastures, where He feeds and nourishes us with His Word and Sacraments.

To hear an in-depth discussion of this Bible account, visit cph.org/podcast and listen to our Seeds of Faith podcast each week.

Lesson 8

The Good Shepherd

John 10:1–18

Connections

Bible Words
[Jesus says,] "I am the good shepherd. I know My own and My own know Me." John 10:14

Faith Word
Shepherd

Hymn
I Am Jesus' Little Lamb (*LSB* 740; CD 3)

Catechism
Apostles' Creed: Second Article

Take-Home Point
Jesus is my Good Shepherd.

1 Opening (15 minutes)

Welcome Time

What you do: Before class, set up two activity areas. In one, put out copies of Activity Page 8A and crayons. Make copies of Activity Page Fun (below and on CD) for parents or classroom helpers. Adjust talk as necessary.

In the other activity area, set out copies of Activity Page 8B, cotton balls, glue sticks, and markers. *Option:* Set out toy farm animals and blocks.

Option: During this time, tape-record each child saying, "I am Jesus' little lamb." Use the recording to introduce the story.

Play the CD from your Teacher Tools to familiarize the children with the hymns and songs. In time, some will even start to hum or sing along. As the children arrive, greet each one. Give them a sticker to put on the attendance chart.

Say **Hi, [Mateas], what did you do this week?** Build relationships with the children by actively listening. Then direct them to an opening activity.

Activity Page Fun Get a copy of Activity Page 8A. Have your child name the items in the boxes and then use a colored marker to draw a line from the sheep to the things it needs. Then use a different color to draw a line from the child to each thing a child needs. Talk about how our needs are similar and how they are different.

Say **Sheep have shepherds who take care of them and give them food and water and a place to live. Jesus takes care of us. He gives us the things we need to live. He died on the cross for us to save us from being punished. He gives us a home in heaven.**

© 2016 Concordia Publishing House. Reproduced by permission. Available on the Teacher CD.

MATERIALS NEEDED

1 Opening	2 God Speaks	3 We Live	4 Closing
Teacher Tools Attendance chart & CD	**Teacher Tools** Poster F	**Student Pack** Craft Page 8 Stickers	**Teacher Tools** CD
Student Pack Attendance stickers	**Student Pack** Lesson Leaflet 8 Little lamb name sticker	**Other Supplies** Sprout Cotton balls Bananas, coconut & plastic forks Activity Page 8C (TG, optional) Paper Plus supplies (optional)	**Student Pack** Take-home items
Other Supplies Activity Pages 8A & 8B (TG) Cotton balls & glue stick Tape recorder (optional) Resource Page 1 (TG, optional) Toy animals & blocks (optional)	**Other Supplies** Scarf or blindfold Optional storytelling props *Jesus, My Good Shepherd* Arch Book (optional)		

Active Learning Have children color the Activity Page 8B and glue cotton balls to its body. As they work, talk about sheep, lambs, and the work of shepherds. *Option:* Set out toy farm animals and blocks for the children to build fences and barns. Have them playact taking care of the animals.

Say **Today in our Bible story, we will hear about lambs and shepherds. Jesus says He is our Good Shepherd.**

Use your signal when it is time to clean up, or sing a cleanup song (Resource Page 1). Cue the children to join you for the opening and story.

Sing **Come and listen to God's Word, to God's Word, to God's Word. Come and listen to God's Word, from His book, the Bible.**

Gathering in God's Name

What you do: Begin with this opening. To teach about the Church Year, use the materials in the Church Year Worship Kit.

Sing "We Are in God's House Today" (*LOSP*, p. 12; CD 15) or another song

Invite the children to say the Invocation and Amen with you. Tell them "Amen" is the special word they get to say at the end of prayers and the like.

Begin **In the name of the Father and of the Son and of the Holy Spirit. Amen.**

Offering Have a child bring the offering basket forward. Sing an offering song.

Pray **Be with us, dear Jesus,* we ask You this day.* Help us to listen,* to learn and obey.* Amen.***

Say as an echo prayer, repeating each phrase at the asterisk.

Celebrate Birthdays, Baptism birthdays, and special occasions

2 God Speaks (20 minutes)

Story Clue

What you do: If the children are not afraid to wear a blindfold, use a scarf for a blindfold. *Option:* If you made a tape recording of the children saying "I am Jesus' little lamb," play it, and let the children guess who is speaking.

Great Multisensory Learning!

Say **Let's play a game to see if you know who is talking, just by listening to the person's voice.**

Ask a child to stand by you and turn around so his back is toward the other children. Have him close his eyes or wear a blindfold. Silently point to another child to say "hello." Have the first child try to guess who was speaking. Repeat so that everyone who wants a turn to guess or speak has a chance to do so.

Say **We did pretty well at recognizing who was talking just by listening to the person's voice without seeing who it was. I know someone who is really super at recognizing voices. He is never wrong.**

Ask **Do you know who that is? Jesus! In our Bible story today, we will hear what Jesus said about knowing someone by the sound of their voice.**

Bible Story Time

What you do: Open your Bible to John 10:1–18. You will also need Poster F. Encourage the children to do sounds and motions with you where indicated.

Storytelling options: (1) Use simple props (a yardstick staff, a towel headpiece, a blanket sheep pen) and act out the part of the shepherd. Have the children pretend they are sheep. (2) Dramatize the story by using blocks to build a sheep pen. Add toy sheep. Have toy people for a shepherd and a robber. (3) Read the Arch Book *Jesus, My Good Shepherd* (CPH, 59-1595).

Key Point

We are like sheep who have gone astray. Jesus is the Good Shepherd who rescues, gathers, and cares for us through His Word and Sacraments.

Say **One day, Jesus was teaching some people. He wanted them to know that He is the Savior God had promised to send. So, He told them a story about a shepherd and some sheep.**

Ask **Do you know what a shepherd is?** Listen to answers.

Say **A shepherd is a person who takes care of sheep. He gives his sheep food to eat and water to drink. He protects his sheep and keeps them safe from other animals that want to hurt them.**

There were many shepherds where Jesus lived. So, the people Jesus was talking to knew all about the important work that shepherds did. Jesus told them this story to help them understand the important work He had come to do.

Let's pretend I am the shepherd and you are the sheep in Jesus' story. Show me how you can "baa," little sheep.

Spread out a blanket for a pretend pen. If you are using blocks and toy sheep, build a sheep pen out of blocks. Have children "baa" for sheep.

Say **Now it's time to settle down for the night.** Have children sit on blanket.

Jesus said that when a shepherd goes to the sheep pen to get his sheep, he goes to the gate of the pen and opens it. Pretend to open a gate. **The shepherd stands at the gate and calls to the sheep, "Come, sheep. Come with me."** Wave hand at sheep. **The shepherd loves his sheep. He knows each one. He calls each sheep by name: "Come on, Suki."** Children "baa." **"Let's go, Stan."** Children "baa."

The sheep know their shepherd's voice too. They hurry to follow him. Lead children or move sheep out of pen. **The shepherd leads the sheep to water and good grass to eat.** Walk one way. **Then he leads them back to the pen for a safe place to sleep.** Walk back to pen.

Does the shepherd have to climb over the wall to get into the pen? Shake head no. **No, someone who does that is trying to steal the sheep from the shepherd. This person does not love the sheep. He won't take care of them. He just wants to hurt them.**

Show Poster F. **Who is this? Yes, it's Jesus. Jesus told those listening to Him, "I am the Good Shepherd. The Good Shepherd lays down His life for the sheep. I take good care of you the same way a good shepherd cares for his sheep. I love you so much that I will die for you."**

Jesus is our Good Shepherd too. He loves us and takes care of us. Jesus loves us so much that He laid down His life for us by dying on the cross to pay for our sins. Jesus keeps us safe from our enemies—sin, death, and the devil. Someday, Jesus will take us to live with Him forever in our home in heaven.

Growing in CHRIST.

Bible Story Review

What you do: Show Poster F and use the questions to review the story. Then hand out Lesson Leaflet 8 and crayons.

Ask **What do we call the person who takes care of sheep?** A shepherd

What does the shepherd do for the sheep? He gives them food and water; he protects them from wild animals; he looks for lost sheep and brings them back to the sheep pen.

Who is our Good Shepherd? Jesus

How does Jesus take care of you? Accept answers.

Direct attention to the leaflet. Point to the three animals in the sidebar.

Say **Jesus is our Good Shepherd. What does He call us?**

Have children circle the picture of the sheep. On side 2, talk about ways Jesus cares for us, and have children circle the pictures that show that.

Option: Do the action poem "Jesus, the Good Shepherd" (*W&W*, p. 110) together, or sing "I Am Jesus' Little Lamb" (*LSB* 740; CD 3).

Bible Words

What you do: You will need the name sticker from the Sticker Page. You may wish to print their names on the stickers ahead of time, or do so as you hand them out. Open your Bible to John 10:14: [Jesus says,] "I am the good shepherd. I know My own and My own know Me."

Say **Show me how these things make you feel by doing thumbs-up** (feel good) **or thumbs-down** (feel bad). Demonstrate the actions.

ice cream on a hot day
a tummy ache
a hug from Mom or Dad
a bee sting

Now, tell me how you feel when you hear these words from the Bible: [Jesus says,] "I am the Good Shepherd. I know My own and My own know Me." Put your thumb up.

These words make me feel great! I am so happy that Jesus is my Good Shepherd. Jesus loves me so much that He died on the cross for me. I know He will always take care of me. Can you echo the words after me?

[Jesus says,]* "I am the good shepherd.* I know My own* and My own* know Me."* Tell the children you have a sticker for them to remind them that they are Jesus' lambs. Say their names as you give each one the sticker.

3 We Live (15 minutes)

Help children grow in their understanding of what the Bible story means for their lives. Choose the activities that work best with your class.

Growing through God's Word

What you do: You will need Sprout and your Bible.

Teacher: Sprout is here. How are you? (*Lead children in saying hi to Sprout.*)

Sprout: Hi, Teacher! Hi, kids! I'm fine today, but something really scary happened to me yesterday.

Teacher: Oh dear, Sprout, what happened?

Sprout: Well, I was at the mall with my dad. I really wanted to go look at the puppies in the pet store window, but my dad said, "No, we don't have time today." So, we just headed to the bookstore. But then my dad took so long there that I decided to go find the puppies by myself.

Teacher: Oh, Sprout, it is not safe for you to go off by yourself like that. You should have stayed with your dad. He must have been worried when he found out you were missing. What happened?

Sprout: Well, I thought I knew the way to the pet store, but everything started looking the same. I couldn't remember where to go. I was so scared. Finally, I stopped and shouted, "Daaaad"! Then I heard my dad's voice calling, "Sprooouut!" I kept calling, and pretty soon my dad came around the corner. Was I glad! He scooped me up in his arms and gave me a big hug.

Teacher: Oh, Sprout, I'm glad your dad found you. I hope you won't wander off like that again!

Sprout: Nope! I learned my lesson. I'm so glad my dad found me! I'm glad he loves me so much. Well, I gotta run. Dad and I are going to read a book.

Say **What happened to Sprout reminds me a little of our Bible story today. Sprout did not listen to His father. He wandered off and got lost. But Sprout's dad loved him and came to find him. Jesus is our Good Shepherd. He loves us and cares for us. He made us His children through Baptism. He talks to us through His Word, the Bible.**

But sometimes we are like Sprout. We don't listen to what our Good Shepherd, Jesus, tells us in His Word. Show Bible. **The wrong things that we think and say and do hurt God and other people. They hurt us too. But Jesus loves us so much that He died on the cross to pay for the wrong things we say and do—our sins. He loves us so much that He forgives us and calls us back to Him through our Baptism and His Word. He helps us want to follow Him and listen to His voice. He cares for us every day. He gives us food and clothes and parents and others to love us. He helps us when we are hurt. Someday, our Good Shepherd will take us to live with Him in heaven!**

Craft Time

What you do: Give the children Craft Page 8, stickers, and crayons to make a stand-up picture of Jesus, our Good Shepherd. For texture, add cotton balls to the lamb in Jesus' arms. Before class, cut off the strip at the top of the Craft Page and cut the slits in the bottom of the Craft Page.

Help the children find side 1 of the Craft Page. Point to the words and read them. Show children how to trace over the letters with a crayon to make the word *Jesus*. The children can color the staff and add sheep stickers to the page. On side 2, read the words.

Ask **Who is Jesus talking about?**

Tell children to color the children to look like them and a friend. Tape the strip of paper in a circle and slip it into the slits in the Craft Page so the Craft

Growing in CHRIST.

Page stands up. *Option:* Glue cotton balls to the lamb in Jesus' arms on side 1 before putting the page into the stand. Talk about ways Jesus, our Good Shepherd, cares for us (e.g., He gives us food; He watches over us; He hears our prayers; He died for us).

Paper Plus options: Make lamb puppets. To make a paper-plate lamb puppet, you will need a copy of Activity Page 8C, two paper plates, and cotton balls for each child. You will also need scissors and glue sticks. Cut out the lamb face and glue it to a plate. Staple this plate to a second plate, leaving an opening at the bottom to insert your hand. Tape over the staples. Glue cotton balls around the lamb's face.

To make sheep sock puppets, use a black sock for each puppet. The toe area of the sock will be the face. Sew on buttons or glue on craft eyes. Glue cotton balls or stuffing around the sock for the sheep's body. Add four black legs and two ears cut from felt.

Snack Time

Make woolly lambs. You will need bananas, coconut, and plastic forks. Slice the bananas and put a fork in each piece. Children press the banana slice in coconut to make a woolly lamb snack.

Live It Out

Make lamb sock puppets (see Paper Plus), or ask the children to bring in gently used Bible story books. Donate the puppets or books to your church's nursery so the little lambs who use that space will learn about Jesus, their Good Shepherd.

4 Closing (5 minutes)

Going Home

What you do: Send home take-home pages and crafts. Cue CD.

Sing "I Am Jesus' Little Lamb" (*LSB* 740; CD 3)

Say **Today, we talked about shepherds taking care of their sheep. Jesus is our Good Shepherd. We are His lambs. Let's say, "Jesus is my Good Shepherd" together.** Do so.

Our Good Shepherd, Jesus, loves us and takes care of us. Tell me one way Jesus takes care of you. Let children tell. **Let's thank Jesus for being our Good Shepherd.**

Pray **Dear Jesus, You are the Good Shepherd and we are Your sheep. Thank You for** (insert ideas children said above). **Amen.**

Reflection

How were you a good shepherd for the children today? Were you aware of their needs? Did you give them your full attention? Ask God to help you find ways to connect with each child as you share the Gospel with His little lambs in the weeks to follow.

Lesson 8

Use a crayon to draw lines from the lamb to the things it needs.
Use a different color to draw lines from the child to what the child needs.

Activity Page 8A *Growing in Christ* Early Childhood © 2008 Concordia Publishing House. Reproduced by permission. This page is available on the Teacher CD.

Activity Page 8B *Growing in Christ*® *Early Childhood* © 2007 Concordia Publishing House. Reproduced by permission. This page is available on the Teacher CD.

Activity Page 8C *Growing in Christ*® Early Childhood © 2007 Concordia Publishing House. Reproduced by permission. This page is available on the Teacher CD.

Preparing the Lesson

Jesus Teaches Us to Pray

Luke 11:1–13; John 16:23–33

Lesson 9

_____

Date of Use

Key Point

Our heavenly Father invites us to pray and promises to hear our prayers for the sake of His Son, Jesus.

Law/**Gospel**

I sin by not trusting God and failing to pray to Him for all things. **God promises to hear and answer my prayers because of His Son, Jesus, and to do what is best and good for me.**

Context

In John 16, Jesus prepares His disciples for His imminent death, resurrection, and return to the Father's right hand. Since He would no longer be with them, Jesus teaches them to exercise their faith in the Father by praying and asking the Father in His (Jesus') name. Since the disciples had already received His grace and mercy, they could rely on and pray to their heavenly Father, especially in times of hardship, sorrow, and persecution.

In Luke 11, the disciples realize that they need to learn to pray, and they ask Jesus to teach them. He, in turn, gives them the Lord's Prayer as the model prayer (Luke 11:1–4)—not only as a pattern for other prayers (see Matthew 6:9), but also as a prayer worthy of repeating word for word (Luke 11:2). Jesus also motivates us to pray by teaching us that God promises to hear and answer our prayers (Luke 11:5–13).

Commentary

Jesus tells His disciples and us to pray in His name. This means much more than merely appending the words "in Jesus' name" to the end of our prayers. Praying "in Jesus' name" means trusting that God will hear our prayers and answer them only because of Jesus and His perfect life and sacrificial death. God hears our prayers not because we are inherently worthy to pray to Him, but because Jesus Christ makes us worthy through His shed blood.

Because Jesus came from the Father, came into the world, and left the world to return to His Father (John 16:28)—referring to His whole work of living, dying, and rising to save us sinners—God counts His believers worthy of praying to Him. The world may give us trials and troubles, but Jesus gives us His peace, which prompts us to exercise our faith by praying to our Father in heaven.

These great passages on prayer not only give us the Lord's Prayer, but they also give us Gospel-driven motivation to pray. Luther said, "Thus you find God's entire will presented here. He surely has no other thoughts toward you in His heart than those shown you in this Lord's Prayer" (AE 24:391).

When we learn to pray, we first learn to pray for what God wants: His name, His kingdom, and His will. Then we learn to ask for our temporal needs: daily bread, forgiveness of sins, protection from temptation, and rescue from evil.

In these passages, our Lord also gives Gospel-driven motivation to pray. God gladly answers the persistent prayer. Even before His believers ask, seek, and knock, God has already promised to give, to be found, and to open the door to His gracious provision in Christ Jesus.

To hear an in-depth discussion of this Bible account, visit cph.org/podcast and listen to our Seeds of Faith podcast each week.

Luther's Works American Edition, vol. 24 © 1961 Concordia Publishing House.

Lesson 9
Jesus Teaches Us to Pray
Luke 11:1–13; John 16:23–33

Connections

Bible Words
Pray for one another.
James 5:16

Faith Word
Pray

Hymn
I Am Jesus' Little Lamb
(*LSB* 740; CD 3)

Catechism
Lord's Prayer (CD 17)

Liturgy
Prayer

Take-Home Point
God hears my prayers.

1 Opening (15 minutes)

Welcome Time

What you do: Before class, set up two activity areas. In one, put out copies of Activity Page 9, stickers, and crayons. Make copies of Activity Page Fun (below and on CD) for parents or classroom helpers. Adjust talk as necessary.

In the other activity area, set out communication devices (e.g., toy phones, old cell phones, walkie-talkies, computer keyboards, paper and pens, and old type-writers. *Option:* Search on YouTube for a video that demonstrates sign language.

Play the CD from your Teacher Tools to familiarize the children with the hymns and songs. As the children arrive, greet each one, have them put their offering in the basket, and give them a sticker to put on the attendance chart.

Say Hi, [Lena], I wonder . . . what are some things you do with your hands? Listen, then direct child to some activities that they can do with their hands.

Activity Page Fun Get a copy of Activity Page 9 and stickers.

Ask What is on this page? Hands **Let's trace around your hand in the empty space.** Do so. **What are some things your hands can do?** Let child tell; then have child color the hands and add stickers.

Say These stickers show children using their hands. Which one shows a child working? (The child helping to wash a car) **Put that on one of the hands on your page.** Continue in the same manner, describing the stickers and putting them on the hands. Point to each scene as you say: **Our hands can work and play and praise and pray! Today, you'll hear more about using your hands to pray.**

© 2016 Concordia Publishing House. Reproduced by permission. Available on the Teacher CD.

MATERIALS NEEDED

1 Opening	2 God Speaks	3 We Live	4 Closing
Teacher Tools Attendance chart & CD	**Teacher Tools** CD	**Student Pack** Craft Page 9 Stickers	**Teacher Tools** CD
Student Pack Attendance stickers Activity Page stickers	**Student Pack** Lesson Leaflet 9 Stickers	**Other Supplies** Sprout Collage items	**Student Pack** Take-home materials
Other Supplies Activity Page 9 (TG) Communication devices Resource Page 1 (TG, optional)	**Other Supplies** Old telephone(s) & other communication devices *The Lord's Prayer* Arch Book (optional)	Yarn Salt play dough (optional) Hug-shaped pretzels Paper strips Paper Plus supplies (optional)	

Active Learning Encourage the children to investigate the communication devices you set out. If you found a good online demonstration of someone using sign language to communicate, show that to the children too. Talk about how we talk with our hands using sign language.

Ask **What would you use to talk to someone? How would send a message? In our Bible story, Jesus tells His helpers how to talk to God.**

At cleanup time, use your classroom signal, or sing a cleanup song (Resource Page 1). Gather the children. Do the actions as you say the words.

Say **I can clap and clap my hands,**
Clap my hands, clap my hands,
I can clap and clap my hands,
Thank You, God, for hands.
I can shake and shake my hands . . .
I can use my hands to hug . . .
I can fold my hands to pray . . .

Gathering in God's Name

What you do: Begin with this opening. To teach about the Church Year, use the materials in the Church Year Worship Kit.

Sing "God, Our Father, Hear Your Children" (*LOSP*, p. 14; CD 9)

Invite the children to say the Invocation and Amen with you. Tell them "Amen" is the special word they get to say at the end of prayers and the like.

Begin **In the name of the Father and of the Son and of the Holy Spirit. Amen.**

Offering Have a child bring the offering basket forward. Sing an offering song.

Ask **Who says "Let us pray" in church?** (Pastor) **When you hear these words, it means we are getting ready to talk to God. What can you do when you hear those words?** (Fold hands, bow heads, listen to the prayer) **You can also pray, "Lord, hear our prayer." Let's practice saying that together.** Do so. **Now let's fold our hands and bow our heads and pray.**

Pray **Dear Jesus, thank You for loving us and coming to be our Savior. Thank You for listening to our prayers. Amen.**

Celebrate Birthdays, Baptism birthdays, and special occasions

② God Speaks (20 minutes)

Story Clue

What you do: Bring an old telephone, play telephone, or cell phone to use, or pretend to use one.

Say **When I want to talk to someone, I call the person on the phone.** Pick up phone. **Today, I want to call my best friend on the phone, but I don't have His number. Do any of you know Jesus' telephone number? I really want to talk to Him today.** Wait for their replies.

Hmm, maybe I should send Him a note instead! What do you think? How can I talk to Jesus? Wait for replies. **Yes! The best way for me to talk to**

21, 17

Jesus is to pray to Him. Jesus taught His disciples a special prayer called the Lord's Prayer. Let's listen and find out what Jesus says about this special prayer.

Bible Story Time

What you do: Tell the Bible story using the script below, or play it on track 21 of the CD. Encourage the children to join in the refrain. Practice ahead of time. *Option:* Tell the story using *The Lord's Prayer* Arch Book (CPH, 59-1575).

Say While He was on earth, Jesus talked to God our heavenly Father in prayer. Before He ate, Jesus looked toward heaven and thanked God for His food. Early in the morning, Jesus prayed and asked God to help Him do His work. Sometimes, Jesus prayed all through the night. Jesus also went to quiet places by Himself and talked to God in prayer. He prayed for His friends. He prayed for God's blessing on little children. He prayed for all people everywhere.

Children's response: We pray, our Father, who art in heaven, hear our prayer.

Jesus' friends saw Him talking to God the Father just as children talk to their father. They saw that talking to God made Jesus happy and helped Him in His work. One day after Jesus finished praying, one of His friends asked Him, "Lord, teach us to pray."

Jesus knew that He would soon leave His friends the disciples and go back to heaven. Jesus wanted them to know that even when He was gone, they could still talk to Him through prayer. So, Jesus taught His friends this prayer. It is called the Lord's Prayer because Jesus, our Lord, taught it.

Children's response: We pray, our Father, who art in heaven, hear our prayer.

Jesus told His friends to begin their prayer by saying, "Our Father, who art in heaven." Jesus wanted them to remember that God is our dear Father. He has made us His dear children through Baptism and His Word.

Fathers love their children and give them what they need. God our heavenly Father can do all things. He cares for us. He wants us to talk to Him in prayer when we are worried or afraid. He wants us to tell Him what makes us happy. He wants us to ask Him for the things we need.

Children's response: We pray, our Father, who art in heaven, hear our prayer.

God can do anything we ask Him to do. He promises to hear and answer our prayers. Sometimes we ask for things that aren't good for us. God doesn't give us these things. He says no to these prayers. That's why Jesus told His friends to pray, "Thy will be done." We can be sure that God our Father will answer our prayers in a way that is best. He will give us what we need.

Children's response: We pray, our Father, who art in heaven, hear our prayer.

Jesus told His friends some other things to pray for. He told them to ask God to give them the food they need for every day. God gives us good things to eat. He also gives us people to take care of us, our clothes, shoes, and all the things we need to live. Jesus told His friends to ask God to forgive the wrong things they said and did and to help them to do what is right. Jesus said they should forgive others just as God forgives them.

Key Point

Our heavenly Father invites us to pray and promises to hear our prayer for the sake of His Son, Jesus.

Growing in Christ

Children's response: We pray, our Father, who art in heaven, hear our prayer.

Many people who believe in Jesus have learned this prayer. We pray this prayer in church and Sunday School. Let's listen to the words of the Lord's Prayer. If you can, pray it with me. If you are telling the story, play the Lord's Prayer on track 17 of the Teacher CD, and sing along.

**Our Father who art in heaven,
hallowed be Thy name,
Thy kingdom come,
Thy will be done on earth as it is in heaven;
give us this day our daily bread;
and forgive us our trespasses
as we forgive those who trespass against us;
and lead us not into temptation, but deliver us from evil.
For Thine is the kingdom and the power and the glory forever and ever.
Amen.**

Bible Story Review

What you do: Hand out Lesson Leaflet 9, stickers, and crayons. Point to the picture on the leaflet, and use the questions to review the story.

Ask **Whom is Jesus talking to?** His disciples

What is Jesus teaching His friends about? He is teaching them the Lord's Prayer.

What does Jesus say you can pray about? We can thank God for all the good things He does for us. We can ask Him for help. We can pray for other people. We can ask Him to forgive us for the wrong things we say and do.

Will God always answer our prayers? Yes, in a way that is best.

Direct attention to the leaflet and the sidebar pictures. Give children stickers of the disciples and Jesus; tell them to look for them in the Bible story picture. On side 2, point to the children, and talk about things we can pray for. Give the children a sticker of praying hands to add to this side. Remind them that we can talk to God about anything.

Option: Do this litany with the children to reinforce that we can pray to God about anything. Lead the children in saying "Our Father, who art in heaven" after each thing you name. If there are specific situations you know of where the children need assurance of Jesus' love, name those too.

When something makes you afraid, you can pray . . .
Children's response: "Our Father, who art in heaven."

When you are playing on the playground, you can pray . . . *Response*
When you are sick, you can pray . . . *Response*
God our Father loves you. He promises to answer your prayers.

Bible Words

What you do: Open your Bible to James 5:16.

Say **The Bible says, "Pray for one another." You can pray to our heavenly Father or to God's Son, Jesus, all the time. You can pray the Lord's Prayer, or you can talk to Jesus in your own words. What are some things you can talk to Jesus about?** Accept answers; then summarize: **You**

can thank Him for all the good things He does for you. You can ask Him for help. You can pray for other people. You can ask Him to forgive the wrong things you say and do.

God promises that He will always listen to our prayers and answer them in a way that is best. Let's say our Bible Words together. Use the Bible rhyme from Wiggle & Wonder (p. 28) to introduce the Bible Words.

Say Here is the Bible God gave to me.   *Open hands like book.*
What does He tell me? Let's look and see.   *Shade eyes with hand.*
God's Word says: *Open hands like book.*
"Pray for   *Fold hands in prayer.*
one another."   *Point to one another.*

3 We Live (15 minutes)

Help children grow in their understanding of what the Bible story means for their lives. Choose the activities that work best with your class.

Growing through God's Word

What you do: Use Sprout the puppet.

Teacher: Hi, Sprout. You look sad. How come?

Sprout: Well, I was just wishing Jesus were still here on earth. I could tell Him when I'm sad or angry or scared. I could ask Him to help me when I have a problem. I could tell Him how much I really love Him!

Teacher: Well, Sprout, even though we can't see Jesus with our eyes the way His friends did, He promises that He is still with us. You can listen to what He says in the Bible. And you can still talk to Jesus and tell Him how much you love Him. You can tell Him what makes you sad. You can ask Him to forgive you when you've been bad and help you when you have troubles. You can ask Him to take care of others. You can talk to Him about everything!

Sprout: I can? How?

Teacher: Boys and girls, tell Sprout how he can talk to Jesus. (*Wait for replies.*) That's right. We talk to Jesus when we pray. He is never too busy to listen.

Sprout: Really? Then I'm going to ask Him for that bike I saw at the store.

Teacher: That's fine, Sprout. But also remember: Jesus promises to hear and answer our prayers, but He doesn't promise to give us everything we ask for! Sometimes Jesus says yes, sometimes He says no, and sometimes He says we have to wait. But He will always answer in a way that's best.

Craft Time

What you do: You will need Craft Page 9, stickers, markers or crayons, yarn, and collage items. Use a paper punch to punch two holes in the top. String yarn through the holes to hang as a banner.

Hand out the Craft Pages with the table prayer facing up. Read the prayer and have the children add a sticker to the end of each line of the prayer. Give them markers and decorating materials to finish coloring and personalizing the page. Say the words again. Use the prayer at snack time, and tell the

Teacher Tip

Very young children will ignore the words when gluing or pasting and cover them up! Be sure to show them the exact area to decorate. Draw some extra lines or *X*s on the paper to help them define the area. This is also useful for any child who is easily distracted visually.

children they can use the prayer before meals at home.

Turn the paper over. Talk about the pictures as you say the words to the Lord's Prayer on this side of the page. Give the children markers, collage items, stickers, and the like to color the border and decorate around the prayer. Make the page into a banner, and encourage the children to hang the prayer in their room and pray the Lord's Prayer at home.

Say   **This is the prayer that Jesus told His friends the disciples to pray. We pray this prayer in church and Sunday School. After you decorate the banner, you can take it home to help you remember this prayer.**

Paper Plus option: Make hand imprints. Give each children a small ball of clay or salt play dough (find recipes online to make your own). Help them flatten it and make their handprint in it, keeping their fingers together, so the print looks like hands folded in prayer. The clay can be air-dried or baked in an oven. Talk about how we fold our hands to pray.

Snack Time

Serve pretzels in the shape of hugs. Talk about how the pretzels can remind us of arms crossed over our heart in prayer. Pray the prayer on the Craft Page prayer card to thank God for your snack.

Live It Out

God hears and answers our prayers! Help children learn to pray for others by making prayer chains. Provide 1½ × 8½-inch strips of colorful paper. Help children print a name of someone for whom they want to pray on each strip. Alternatively, they can draw a picture of the person or a prayer request.

Show them how to make the first strip into a loop and tape it closed, then connect the remaining strips to make a paper chain. Tell them they can remove a link on the chain each day and pray for the person named on it. Brainstorm prayer requests (e.g., ask for help, give thanks, show love).

4 Closing (5 minutes)

Going Home

What you do: Send home take-home pages and crafts. Cue CD.

Say   **Today, we learned that our heavenly Father invites us to pray and promises to hear us. Let's say "God hears my prayers" together.** Do so. **God will answer your prayers in a way that's best.**

Sing   "Jesus Listens When I Pray" (*LOSP*, p. 15), "God, Our Father, Hear Your Children" (*LOSP*, p. 14; CD 9), or "I Am Jesus' Little Lamb" (*LSB* 740; CD 3)

Pray   **Dear Jesus, thank You for teaching us how to pray. Thank You for answering our prayers in a way that is best for us. In Your name we pray. Amen.**

Reflection

Do the children seem to understand that God hears and answers all our prayers? When you pray next week, remind them of today's lesson and assure them that God is listening to that prayer too.

Lesson 9

My Hands Can Work and Play and Praise and Pray

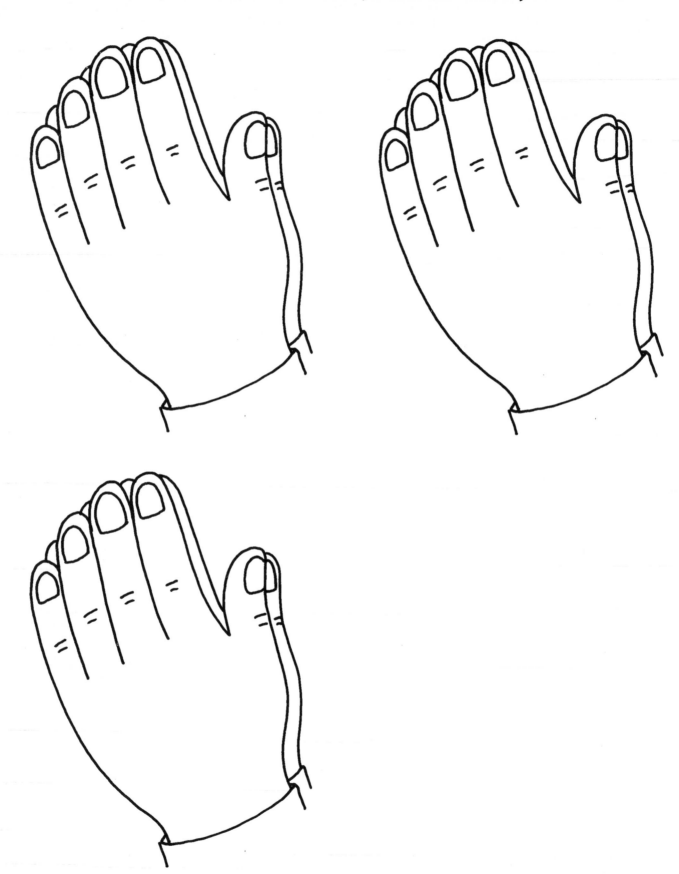

In the space, trace around child's hand. Add stickers to show ways we use our hands.

Activity Page 9 Growing in Christ® Early Childhood © 2007 Concordia Publishing House. Reproduced by permission. This page is available on the Teacher CD.

Preparing the Lesson

_____

Jesus Raises Lazarus

John 11:1–45

Key Point

In resurrecting Lazarus, Jesus demonstrated that He can indeed raise all who believe in Him for salvation. True life is eternal life with Jesus.

Law/**Gospel**

In this life, I see and experience the effects of sin: sickness, injury, and death. **Jesus, who is the source of all life, will raise me and all who believe in Him to life with Him forever, where there will be no more death or mourning or crying or pain.**

Context

The ultimate purpose of Jesus' earthly ministry is drawing near. Jesus has spent time among the people of Galilee and Judea, teaching and healing them. Now, He goes to Jerusalem to die. It is important to notice that this miracle of restoring life leads into the sacrificial death of Jesus during Passover (John 11:55–12:1).

Commentary

John links miracles to spiritual truth throughout his Gospel, sometimes connecting them to Jesus'"I am" sayings (e.g., the feeding of the five thousand in chapter 6 and the healing of the man born blind in chapter 9). The miracles are not mere symbols, for in heaven we will eat real food and will see with our perfected eyes; yet the miracles also show that Jesus is our spiritual food and our spiritual focus.

In resurrecting Lazarus, Jesus shows that He will indeed raise up all the dead and that true life is eternal life with Him (11:23–26). When we see things from the perspective of eternity, we believe that all things will work for God's glory and good, even if we do not understand everything now.

This miracle is "so that the Son of God may be glorified through it" (v. 4). Yet, the glory of God is not just showing His power and might over and against this world. Rather, the glorification of Jesus is His death on the cross for the life of the world (12:23, 27–28). By dying and rising, Jesus overcomes the power that death has over us. In His great act of suffering, shame, and humiliation, God is actually glorified, for in it He accomplishes His greatest work: the salvation of humankind.

By raising Lazarus, Jesus causes enough political stir that the religious establishment seeks from then on to kill Him, eventually leading to His crucifixion (11:53). Indeed, that Jesus dies to give us eternal life is climactically prophesied by the high priest Caiaphas himself (vv. 49–52).

Thus, the raising of Lazarus foreshadows Jesus' giving up His own life that we might live. Jesus returns to Judea to raise Lazarus, knowing that the Jews are seeking to put Him to death (vv. 7–8), yet doing so because He must finally die so that all, not just Lazarus, may rise.

To hear an in-depth discussion of this Bible account, visit cph.org/podcast and listen to our Seeds of Faith podcast each week.

Lesson 10
Jesus Raises Lazarus
John 11:1–45

Connections

Bible Words
[Jesus says,] "Because I live, you also will live."
John 14:19

Faith Word
Eternal life

Hymn
Have No Fear, Little Flock
(*LSB* 735; CD 1)

Catechism
Apostles' Creed:
Second Article

Take-Home Point
Jesus gives me life with Him forever.

 Opening (15 minutes)

Welcome Time

What you do: Before class, set up two activity areas. In one, put out copies of Activity Page 10A and crayons. Make copies of Activity Page Fun (below and on CD) for parents or classroom helpers. Adjust talk as necessary.

In the other activity area, set out a variety of magnets with items that they attract (paper clips, refrigerator magnets, magnetic letters, etc.).

Play the CD from your Teacher Tools to familiarize the children with the hymns and songs. As the children arrive, greet each one, have them put their offerings in the basket, and give each a sticker to put on the attendance chart.

Say Hi, [Jack], I wonder . . . can you make a muscle arm? Demonstrate. **You are strong! Today, we're going to learn about God's power!**

Activity Page Fun Get a copy of the Activity Page. Help your child find the items from the top row in the picture below it.

Ask When you are sick, what helps you get better? Let child tell. **God gives us doctors and medicine to help us get better. Today, you will hear about a man who was so sick that doctors could not make him better. Jesus used His power to do something no one else can do!**

© 2016 Concordia Publishing House. Reproduced by permission. Available on the Teacher CD.

MATERIALS NEEDED

1 Opening	2 God Speaks	3 We Live	4 Closing
Teacher Tools Attendance chart & CD	**Teacher Tools** Storytelling Figures 10-1 to 10-7 Backgrounds A & B	**Teacher Tools** Craft Page 10 Stickers	**Teacher Tools** CD
Student Pack Attendance stickers	**Student Pack** Lesson Leaflet 10	**Other Supplies** Sprout Magnet & magnetic items Pretzel sticks or crackers & pressurized cheese *What Happened When Grandma Died?* book (optional) Paper Plus supplies (optional)	**Student Pack** Take-home items
Other Supplies Activity Page 10A (TG) Magnets & magnetic items Resource Page 1 (TG, optional)	**Other Supplies** Activity Page 10B (TG) Dead plant (optional) *Get Up, Lazarus!* Arch Book (optional)		

Active Learning Encourage children to use the magnets with the items you set out. Talk about the power that magnets have to pick up some objects.

Say **Magnets have power to pick up some objects. In our Bible story today, Jesus shows His power. He does something only God can do. He makes someone who is dead come alive again.**

Use your classroom signal when it is time to clean up. Sing a cleanup song (Resource Page 1). Cue the children to join you for the opening and story.

Sing **Come and listen to God's Word, to God's Word, to God's Word. Come and listen to God's Word, from His book, the Bible.**

Gathering in God's Name

What you do: Gather the children, and begin with this opening. To teach about the Church Year, use the materials in the Church Year Worship Kit.

Sing "God, Our Father, Hear Your Children" (*LOSP*, p. 14; CD 9) or another song

Invite the children to say the Invocation and Amen with you. Tell them "Amen" is the special word they get to say at the end of prayers and the like.

Begin **In the name of the Father and of the Son and of the Holy Spirit. Amen.**

Offering Have a child bring the offering basket forward. Sing an offering song.

Pray **Dear Jesus, we are glad You love us. We are glad You understand all our feelings, even sad ones. We are glad we will live with You in heaven. Help us listen and learn more about You and Your love for us. Amen.**

Celebrate Birthdays, Baptism birthdays, and special occasions

2 God Speaks (20 minutes)

Story Clue

What you do: Copy and fold Activity Page 10B in half so children see one picture at a time. Show the plant picture, or bring a dead-looking plant to show.

Ask **How does this plant look?** Accept all answers. **Yes, it looks droopy. It has broken stems, and the leaves have holes. It is a sick plant. What could we do to help this plant?** Accept all answers—water it; place it in sun; nothing because it is already dead. **What will happen to it if it doesn't get enough water or sunshine or food to help it get better? Yes, it will die.**

Show second picture on Activity Page 10B. **I wonder what is wrong with the little child?** Accept answers. **What do you think the mom will do?** Accept all answers. **What happens when you get sick? God gives us doctors and medicine to help make us better, doesn't He? In our Bible story today, a man is so sick that the doctors cannot make him better. Jesus uses His power to do an amazing thing. Let's listen and find out what He did.**

Key Point

In resurrecting Lazarus, Jesus demonstrated that He can indeed raise all who believe in Him for salvation. True life is eternal life with Jesus.

Bible Story Time

What you do: Use Backgrounds A and B and Storytelling Figures 10-1 to 10-7. Use a restickable glue stick, double-sided tape, or loops of tape to attach the figures to the background when you tell the story. Keep the children involved by encouraging them to do the story actions with you. Allow them to place story figures on the board.

Have your Bible open to John 11, and tell the children that this is a true story from God's Word. *Option:* Show the pictures and tell the story using the Arch Book *Get Up, Lazarus!* (CPH, 59-1568).

Say   **The Bible tells us about two sisters named Mary and Martha.** Place Mary (10-2) and Martha (10-1) on Background A. **They were good friends of Jesus and liked to do things for Him. Mary and Martha also had a brother. His name was Lazarus** (LAZ ah russ). **Mary and Martha and Lazarus loved Jesus. Jesus loved and cared about them too.**

One day, Lazarus got sick. Mary and Martha were sad and worried. Encourage children to make sad faces and rub eyes. **They sent a man to tell their friend Jesus. They knew that if Jesus were there, He could help their brother. Run, run, run.** Run in place. **The man hurried off to find Jesus.** Remove Mary and Martha. Place Jesus (10-5) and the disciples (10-7) on Background A. **When the man found Jesus, the man said, "Jesus, Your friend Lazarus is sick. Come quickly!" But Jesus had a better plan, so He did not go right away. He stayed where He was for two more days.** Have children hold up two fingers.

Then Jesus said to His friends the disciples, "Lazarus is dead. It is time to go see him." When Martha heard that Jesus was coming, she ran to meet Him. Run, run, run. Run in place. Remove disciples, and add Martha (10-1). **She said, "Oh, Jesus, it is so sad. Lazarus is dead."** Make sad face and rub eyes.

Jesus said, "Your brother will live again. Whoever believes in Me will never really die."

Martha replied, "Yes, I know he will come alive on the Last Day and live in heaven."

Jesus told her, "I am the resurrection and the life. That means I am the one who gives people life again. Do you believe this?"

Martha smiled and said, "Yes, I believe You are the Son of God who has come to save us!" Smile.

Remove figures. **Then Martha hurried to tell Mary that Jesus was coming. Run, run, run.** Run in place. **When Mary heard that, she went to meet Jesus and fell at His feet.** Add Jesus (10-5) and Mary (10-2). **She said, "Lord, if You had been here, our brother would not have died."** Remove figures; turn to Background B.

Mary, Martha, and their friends took Jesus to the place where Lazarus was buried. Place Jesus (10-5) on right side of board. Put Mary (10-2), Martha (10-1), and crowd (10-3) on left side of Background B. Add disciples (10-7). **The people were sad. Some of them were crying.** Make sad faces and rub eyes. **Jesus felt sad too. He cried. There was a big stone in front of the place where Lazarus was buried.** Place stone (10-6) in front of tomb. **Jesus said, "Take away the stone."**

Growing in CHRIST

The people did what Jesus said and took away the stone. Remove stone (10-6). **Jesus prayed to His Father in heaven, "Thank You for hearing Me, Father."** Fold hands and look up. **Then Jesus said in a loud voice, "Lazarus, come out!"**

Step, step, step. Step in place. **Lazarus came out!** Add Lazarus (10-4). **He wasn't dead anymore. Jesus had made him alive again! Mary smiled. Martha smiled. The people around them smiled.** Smile.

When Jesus brought Lazarus back to life, He showed His power over sin and death. He showed that He is the Savior God promised to send. Jesus cares for us too. He came to die on the cross to pay for our sins. He promises to give all those who believe in Him life with Him forever.

Bible Story Review

What you do: Hand out Lesson Leaflet 10 and crayons or markers. Use the review questions to check for comprehension.

Ask **Who are the two women?** Mary and Martha

How do they feel at the beginning of the story? They are sad.

What did Jesus do? He brought their brother, Lazarus, back to life.

What will Jesus do for us one day? Jesus will give us and all who believe in Him eternal life.

Have the children look at the pictures in the sidebar and describe what is happening. Tell them to write numbers to show the sequence of story events. On side 2, have them draw mouths on Mary and Martha to show how they felt when Jesus raised Lazarus back to life.

Option: Retell the Bible story, and have children pantomime the characters' actions.

Bible Words

What you do: Have your Bible open to John 14:19.

Say **A miracle is something special that happens by God's power. What miracle did Jesus do in our Bible story this week that shows He is God?** (He raised Lazarus back to life, something only God can do.) **Jesus is God's Son. He has power over death.**

Jesus came to be our Savior. He died on the cross to pay for our sins. But on Easter, He came back to life again. He tells us, "Because I live, you also will live." Someday, all those who believe in Jesus as their Savior will live with Him in heaven. Jesus gives us eternal life. Let's say our Bible Words together.

Divide the children into two groups. Lead each group in saying their part of the verse. Say the verse a few times; then, switch parts.

Say Group 1: [**Jesus says,**] **"Because I live,**
Group 2: **you also will live."**

3 We Live (15 minutes)

Help children grow in their understanding of what the Bible story means for their lives. Choose the activities that work best with your class.

Growing through God's Word

What you do: You will need Sprout. Put a magnet and a few magnetic items inside Sprout's backpack (e.g., paper clips, a washer, a refrigerator magnet), or use a battery-operated or paper fan and have a few lightweight objects for the fan to blow away. If your puppet does not have a backpack, put the items in a paper lunch bag. Adapt the script accordingly.

Sprout: Hi, Teacher. Hi, kids. I have something special in my backpack. May I show you?

Teacher: Sure, Sprout. Let me help you get it out. (*Take out magnet and items.*)

Sprout: (*Demonstrating how magnet works*) Look, I can pick up these paper clips without even using my hands. Isn't that cool? What makes it do that?

Teacher: That is pretty awesome, Sprout! The magnet has power to make things come to it. We call that magnetic attraction.

Sprout: I wonder what else my magnet can pick up. (*Demonstrates picking up other magnetic objects*) Look! My magnet can pick up all these things! (*Tries it on a book or teacher*) But I can't get it to work on this book—or on you!

Teacher: (*Laughing*) No, Sprout. Magnets only have power to pick up certain things. That's how God has made them. Only God has power to do whatever He wants just by saying the word. Do you remember how God made the world? Did He get a hammer and some wood?

Sprout: (*Chuckling*) No, God just said, "Let it be."

Teacher: That's right, Sprout! God spoke His powerful Word, and right away, sky and plants and animals appeared. God makes the wind blow and the snow fall. He makes babies grow. He even makes dead things alive again.

Sprout: Wow! God sure has a lot of power!

Teacher: Yes, He does. The Bible tells us that God is all powerful. In today's Bible story, Jesus showed His power. When Jesus brought Lazarus back to life, He showed that He is God's Son and our promised Savior. Jesus has all power. He has power over sin, death, and the devil. He died on the cross to pay for our sins, and He rose again on Easter. He promises that someday He will take us to live with Him in heaven.

Sprout: Wow! I'm glad Jesus loves me and came to be my Savior. I love Him too!

Craft Time

What you do: Give children Craft Page 10 and the stone and flower stickers. Set out scissors, tape or glue, and crayons to use. Have helpers on hand, or cut out pieces and prefold the page before class.

Have the children identify the characters from today's Bible story. They can color the story characters and the flowers. Give them a stone sticker to put on the dashed outline and flower stickers to add wherever they wish.

Active Learning Idea!

Then, tell them to cut the characters apart and fold back the bottoms on the dotted lines. Help them cut and fold the pop-up tab. Tape or glue Lazarus to the pop-up tab. Glue Jesus and the sisters somewhere in the foreground.

Paper Plus option: Plant bean seeds in individual paper cups filled halfway with soil or in plastic zipper bags with damp paper towels inside of them. The beans go between the damp towels and the side of the plastic bag. Talk about how the seeds do not look alive, but God has power to make them grow into plants. Place the seeds in the sunshine, and be sure to water them to keep the soil or towels moist. As the beans sprout, discuss how God brings new life.

Snack Time

Give children stick pretzels to make crosses, or serve crackers. Use a can of pressurized cheese to make crosses on the crackers. Talk about how Jesus died on the cross and rose again to give us life with Him forever.

Option: Search online for a video that shows the life cycle of a caterpillar to butterfly. Watch it as the children eat their snack. Use the video to talk about how something that looks dead emerges into new life. The butterfly can remind us of our new life with Jesus.

Live It Out

Read the book *What Happened When Grandma Died* by Peggy Barker (CPH, 561458WEB), which explains to young children what happens when God calls a loved one home to heaven. Allow time for the children to express their feelings about sickness and death. Assure them that Jesus cares for them in this life and has made it possible for them to have life with Him forever. Talk about ways they can show love for those who are sad.

4 Closing (5 minutes)

Going Home

What you do: Have take-home pages, your CD player, and CD nearby.

Sing "Do You Know Who Died for Me" (*LOSP*, p. 93; CD 7) or "Have No Fear, Little Flock" (*LSB* 735; CD 1)

Say **When Jesus brought Lazarus back to life, He showed His power over sin and death. He showed that He is the Savior God promised to send. God forgives our sins and gives eternal life to everyone who believes in Jesus. Let's say "Jesus gives me life with Him forever."** Do so.

Pray Lead the children in this prayer litany:

Dear Jesus, You help us every day. Children: Thank You, Jesus.
You heal us when we're sick. Children: Thank You, Jesus.
You wash away our sins. Children: Thank You, Jesus.
You will take us to heaven someday. Children: Thank You, Jesus.
Amen. Children: Amen.

Reflection

Were there opportunities for the children to express their feelings about sickness and death? Let your pastor know if some were especially bothered. Think of ways you can continue to share with them the joy that Jesus gives.

Find and circle all the things doctors use to help us get better.

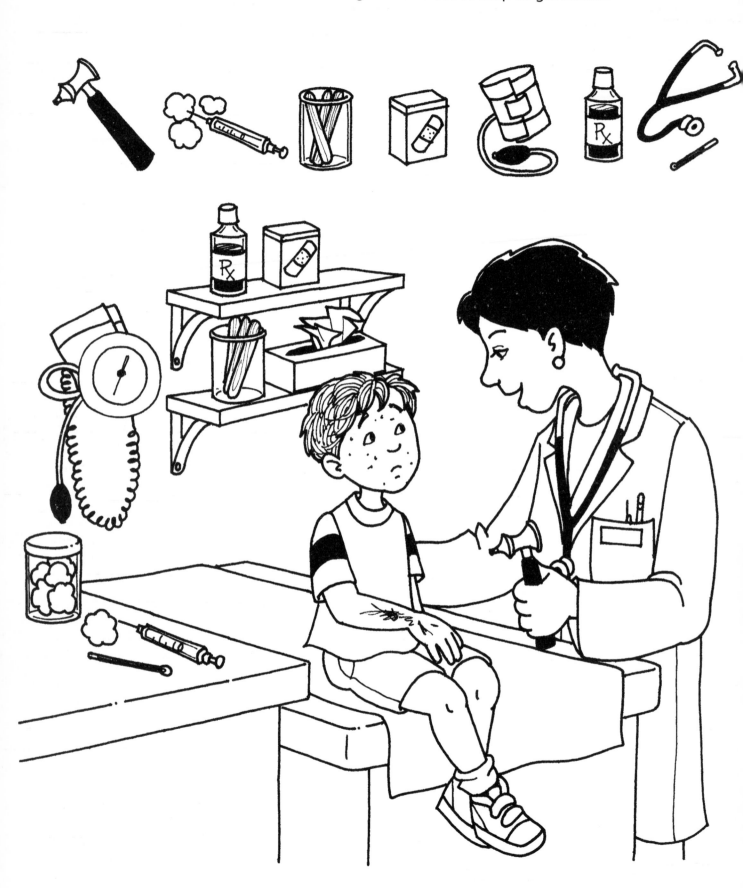

Activity Page 10A Growing in Christ® Early Childhood © 2008 Concordia Publishing House. Reproduced by permission. This page is available on the Teacher CD.

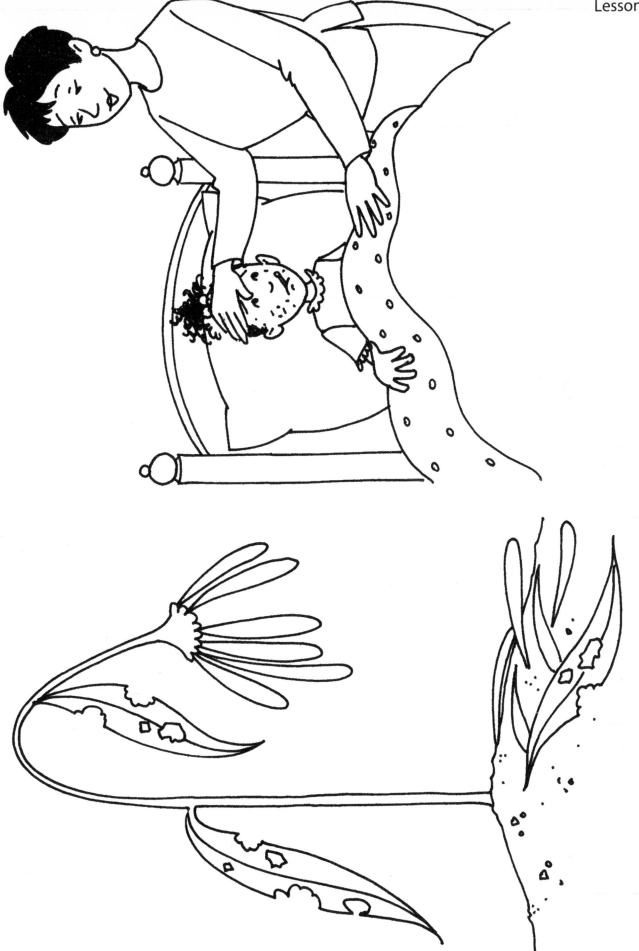

Activity Page 10B *Growing in Christ®* Early Childhood © 2008 Concordia Publishing House. Reproduced by permission. This page is available on the Teacher CD.

Preparing the Lesson

Jesus Seeks the Lost

Luke 15

_____

Key Point

In our sin, we were lost from God and doomed to die. God, in His love, sought and found us and keeps us with Him forever.

Law/Gospel

Because of my sin, I am lost from God. **My heavenly Father does not abandon me, but seeks me out through His Word and Sacraments, forgives me completely for Jesus' sake, and keeps me safe in faith.**

Context

A parable is an earthly story with a heavenly meaning. It uses simple figures and illustrations from everyday life in which deep spiritual thoughts are conveyed. When the Pharisees chided Jesus for welcoming the outcasts—the rejected sinners, the dregs of society—Jesus used parables to show where they were wrong and God was right.

Commentary

We cannot be so bad that Christ's forgiveness does not reach us. We can be sure of God's love. The only unpardonable sin (Matthew 12:31–32) is that against the Holy Spirit, whereby one strongly claims that the work of Christ, and thus, the Holy Spirit, is really of the devil. Such high blasphemy does not come from forgiven sinners but rather from people like the unforgiving brother of the prodigal son.

Since God goes to such lengths for us, we realize, unlike the unforgiving brother, that forgiveness is God's business to create through His Means of Grace, God's Word and the Sacraments, and not ours to regulate with our own aesthetics and ideas of works-righteousness. With God and the holy angels, we rejoice when even one sinner repents and comes to salvation through Word and Sacrament. We can be sure that God's love finds us and forgives us completely through the suffering and death of Jesus Christ, given to us in the Means of Grace.

These parables have one point: God loves you so much that He will move heaven and earth to have you as His own. If you lose your way, God will seek and find you. If you play the fool, wasting your life away in carnal pleasures as a prodigal son or daughter, your heavenly Father will still receive you and your broken, penitent heart.

In addition, God will let no one prevail against you, a penitent sinner who—though declared righteous for Jesus' sake—still feels unworthy and desires that God not soil Himself by coming into contact with you. Instead, you become a new creation in Christ who praises God.

To hear an in-depth discussion of this Bible account, visit cph.org/podcast and listen to our Seeds of Faith podcast each week.

Lesson 11

Jesus Seeks the Lost

Luke 15

Connections

Bible Words
The Son of Man came to seek and to save the lost. Luke 19:10 (CD 5)

Faith Word
Repent

Hymn
Have No Fear, Little Flock (*LSB* 735; CD 1)

Catechism
Baptism

Liturgy
Confession and Absolution

Take-Home Point
God is my loving, forgiving Father.

 1 Opening (15 minutes)

Welcome Time

What you do: Before class, set up two activity areas. In one, put out copies of Activity Page 11A and crayons. Make copies of Activity Page Fun (below and on CD) for parents or classroom helpers. Adjust talk as necessary.

In the other activity area, have several pieces of fruit and two bowls. You will also need a paring knife, for adult use only. Do not set it out ahead of time. Use it or have a helper use it and then put it away.

Play the CD from your Teacher Tools. Greet the children, have them put their offering in the basket, and give them a sticker to put on the attendance chart.

Say Hi, [Camilla], what is your favorite animal on the farm? Today, we'll hear about someone who had to feed the pigs.

Activity Page Fun Get a copy of Activity Page 11A. Show the page to your child.

Ask What do you think the people are celebrating? Accept answers. **In our Bible story today, a father is so happy that he has a party for his son. Listen to the story and find out why he is happy. You can tell me about it later.**

© 2016 Concordia Publishing House. Reproduced by permission. Available on the Teacher CD.

MATERIALS NEEDED

1 Opening	2 God Speaks	3 We Live	4 Closing
Teacher Tools Attendance chart & CD	**Teacher Tools** Storytelling Figures 11-1 to 11-4 Background A & CD	**Student Pack** Craft Page 11 Stickers	**Teacher Tools** CD
Student Pack Attendance stickers	**Student Stuff** Lesson Leaflet 11	**Other Supplies** Activity Page 11B (TG) & paper cups	**Student Pack** Take-home materials
Other Supplies Activity Page 11A (TG) Fruit, bowls & knife Resource Page 1 (TG, optional)	**Other Supplies** Story bag with party favors Paper plates Cups, dishpan of sand & toy pigs (optional) *The Parable of the Prodigal Son Arch Book* (optional)	Cupcakes & sprinkles Fruit kabobs Activity Page 11C (optional) Yarn or ribbon (optional) Paper Plus supplies (optional)	

Active Learning Make pig food. Show the fruit you set out, and tell the children that you're going to make a delicious snack for today. Peel and talk about the fruit as they watch. Put the fruit in one bowl and the peels in another bowl. Talk to the children as you peel the fruit.

Say In our Bible story today, a young man leaves home and spends all his money on parties. Soon he has no money for food, so he gets a job feeding pigs. He is so hungry that he thinks the pig food looks good. Show the children the bowl of fruit peels. **This is what the pigs ate. How would you like to eat this?** Accept answers. Save the fruit for your snack.

Use your classroom signal when it is time to clean up. Sing a cleanup song (Resource Page 1). Cue the children to join you for the opening and story.

Sing **Come and listen to God's Word, to God's Word, to God's Word. Come and listen to God's Word, from His book, the Bible.**

Gathering in God's Name

What you do: Gather the children, and begin with this opening. To teach about the Church Year, use the materials in the Church Year Worship Kit.

Sing "God, Our Father, Hear Your Children" (*LOSP*, p. 14; CD 9) or another song

Invite the children to say the Invocation and Amen with you. Tell them "Amen" is the special word they get to say at the end of prayers and the like.

Begin **In the name of the Father and of the Son and of the Holy Spirit. Amen.**

Say **God loves us and forgives us. When we go to church to worship Jesus, we tell God we are sorry for the bad things we think and say and do. We ask Him to forgive us. Then the pastor tells us God forgives us for Jesus' sake. What else do we do in church?** Listen to answers. **Later in the church service, we give an offering. Let's do that now.**

Offering Have a child bring the offering basket forward. Sing an offering song.

Pray **Dear Lord,* You love us all the time.***
You love us when we're good.*
You love us when we're bad.*
You forgive us for Jesus' sake.*
Thank You, God.* Amen.*

*Have children echo each phrase at the asterisk.

Celebrate Birthdays, Baptism birthdays, and special occasions

2 God Speaks (20 minutes)

Story Clue

What you do: Put party favors (e.g., noisemakers, a party hat, birthday candles) in a story bag or paper bag. Use an excited tone of voice.

Ask **What do you think I have in my story bag today?**

Listen to ideas from the children. Have the children come up one at a time, reach into the bag, and guess, just by touch, what the items are.

Say Those were good guesses. Let's see what's inside! Take the items out, and let the children name them. **What could we use all of these things for? That's right! A party! These are party favors! Why do we have parties? Yes, we have parties when we want to celebrate something special. In our Bible story today, a father has a party for his son to show how happy he was. Let's find out why the father was so happy.**

Bible Story Time

What you do: Use Storytelling Figures 11-1 to 11-4 and Background A to teach the story. Also, draw a large happy face on one side of a paper plate and a sad face on the other side, or have the children show you their own happy or sad expressions, as indicated.

Options: Tape the figures to upside-down paper cups. Use them with a dishpan of sand, or set them on a child-size table. Add additional toy pigs. Or tell the story using the Arch Book *The Parable of the Prodigal Son* (CPH, 59-2224).

Say **Jesus wanted everyone to know how much God loves us. One day, He told this story: A father had two sons. They made him so happy.** Show happy face. **Can you show me your happy faces? The younger son said, "Give me my share of the money, Father. I am tired of living here. I want to go someplace where I can play and not work."** Add son and father (11-1) to Background or sand.

The father loved his son. It made him feel sad that his son wanted to leave home. Hold up sad face. **Show me your sad faces. But the father gave his son the money. The young man went far away to another country. He spent all his money on foolish things.** Show sad face again. **Soon, he didn't even have money for food!**

The son got very hungry. Rub stomach. **The only job he could find was taking care of pigs.** Replace 11-1 with son feeding pigs (11-2). **He was so hungry that he wanted to eat the pigs' food!**

One day, the son was watching the pigs eat. He was lonely and sad. Show sad face. **He thought about how much his father loved him. He remembered his nice home. He thought, "I will go home and tell my father I'm sorry for doing wrong things."** Remove son feeding pigs (11-2).

When the father saw his son coming down the road, he was so happy! Show happy face. **The father ran to his son and hugged and kissed him!** Add father greeting son (11-3). **The son said, "I'm sorry, Father. I've done many wrong things. I'm not good enough to be your son."** Show sad face.

The father did not scold him. Instead, he gave him some gifts: a new ring and clothes and sandals. Then the father threw a big party to welcome him back. There was good food and special music and dancing. The father said, "My lost son has come back home! I love him. I am so happy he has come back." Show happy face.

But not everyone in the family was happy. Remember, the father had two sons. Replace figure 11-3 with father and older son (11-4). **The older son was angry and hurt.** Show sad face. **"Why are you having a party?" he asked. "My brother went away. He did bad things. He doesn't deserve a party! That's not fair!"**

The father loved this son too. He said, "Son, your brother has learned an important lesson; I will always love him. I will always love you too.

Key Point

In our sin, we were lost from God and doomed to die. God, in His love, sought and found us and keeps us with Him forever.

Come and celebrate with us." Show happy face.

What a special story! One son went away and did many bad things, but his father still loved him. The other son was angry, but his father still loved him. We think and say and do wrong things too. We call that sin. But God still loves us. He loved us so much that He sent His Son, Jesus, to pay for our sins by dying on the cross. Because of Jesus, someday we will live with Him forever in heaven. That's a lot of love! Show happy face.

Bible Story Review

What you do: Hand out Lesson Leaflet 11 and crayons. Point to the picture on the leaflet as you ask the review questions:

Ask **Where did the son go?** To a faraway land

What are the father and son in the picture doing? The son is returning home; the father has run out to welcome him.

Are they happy or sad? The son is sad and hungry. He may be wondering if his father still loves him. The father is happy. He has been waiting for his son to come back.

Say **God loves us all the time. How does that make you feel? Happy or sad?** Show the happy and sad faces, and accept answers. **God is always willing to forgive us when we do things that are wrong. How does that make you feel?** Show faces again.

Have children look at the sidebar pictures, and circle the son. Then have them trace the dots on the heart and write their name or draw their face in the heart.

On side 2 of the leaflet, talk about how we know God loves us. (He tells us in His Word; He makes us His children through Baptism; He sent Jesus to take our punishment on the cross and forgives us for His sake.) Have kids connect the dots and color the pictures. Sing the song on the leaflet.

Bible Words

What you do: Read the Bible Words from Luke 19:10 in the Bible. Play them on the CD, or have the children say them with the motions to learn the words.

Say **In our Bible story, the father welcomed his son home. He was so happy that he threw a party for him. God loves us even more than this father loved his son. He sent His Son, Jesus, to pay for our sins by dying on the cross and rising again.**

The Bible calls Jesus "the Son of Man." It says, "The Son of Man came to seek and to save the lost." Jesus came from heaven to save us. God, our heavenly Father, welcomes us into His family because of Jesus. He makes us His children in Baptism. Someday, He will welcome us to our home in heaven. God loves us so much! He is so good to us. Let's say the Bible Words together.

Say the Bible Words while passing the happy face from one child to the next. Each time the face goes to a new child, lead children in saying the next word of the verse. Repeat verse at the end. *Option:* Play the verse on track 5 of the CD; then have the children sing along.

(3) We Live (15 minutes)

Help children grow in their understanding of what the Bible story means for their lives. Choose the activities that work best with your class.

Growing through God's Word

What you do: Copy, color, and cut out the figures on Activity Page 11B. Attach each one to an upside-down paper cup. Use the puppets to talk about sinful behaviors and God's forgiveness. Put the Jesus puppet on the table, or hold it in one hand. Hold up the boy puppet in the other hand.

Say **This is Marcos. He was mad at his older brother, so he went into his brother's room and messed it up. Was that a good thing to do? No. Marcos knew he had done something wrong. He felt sad and far away from Jesus.** Move boy puppet away from Jesus puppet. **What should Marcos do? Yes, Marcos needs to tell his brother, "I'm sorry." He needs to ask Jesus to forgive him. And that's just what he did. When Marcos told his brother he was sorry, his big brother gave him a hug and said, "I forgive you." Jesus forgives Marcos too.** Move Jesus puppet close to boy puppet. **Jesus loves Marcos so much that He paid for the wrong things Marcos does—all his sins—on the cross.**

Hold up girl puppet. **This is Talia. Talia's mother told her not to touch her makeup. God wants us to obey our parents. But it's hard to do the right thing all the time, isn't it? Talia didn't obey her mom. She got lipstick all over her mom's new towels. Was that a good thing to do? No. Talia knew she shouldn't have done that. She felt sad and far away from Jesus.** Move girl puppet away from Jesus puppet. **Talia told her mom, "I'm sorry." Her mother was not happy at what Talia did. But she loves Talia! She said, "I forgive you. Jesus forgives you too."** Move Jesus puppet close to girl puppet.

Marcos and Talia did wrong things. They sinned. We all think and say and do wrong things too. But God loves us. He sent Jesus to die on the cross to pay for our sins. He makes us His children in Holy Baptism. He helps us to be sorry and ask for forgiveness. Hold up Jesus puppet. **He tells us in His Word, "I still love you. I forgive you."**

Every week when we go to church, God tells us how much He loves us. He tells us that in His Word, the Bible. He tells us that in Baptism and in the Lord's Supper. He is our loving, forgiving Father.

Craft Time

What you do: You need Craft Page 11, markers, and stickers. *Option:* Make the page into a banner by punching two holes in the top and stringing with yarn or ribbon.

Point out how raggedy the son looks; then give the children stickers of new clothes and sandals to put on the son. Have them draw a ring.

Turn the Craft Page over. Help the children cut apart the strip of pictures on the right. Tell them to glue each picture to the gift box with the matching color and then to color the gift bows. Read the sentences below each gift box. Talk about how God gives us the gifts of forgiveness and eternal life with Him through Jesus. As you talk about the pictures, have the children color the water and shell for Baptism, connect the dots of the Bible, add a sticker of stained glass windows to the church, and color a child with Jesus in heaven.

Ask the children what they see between the gifts. Have them use their finger to trace the space to reveal a cross; then color it. Have Jesus stickers ready to hand out.

Say   **The son in the Bible story left home and did some bad things. But his father still loved him and welcomed him home. We do wrong things too. But God helps us to be sorry. He promises to forgive us for Jesus' sake. Let's add a sticker of Jesus to remind us of God's love.**

Paper Plus option: Help the children make party hats following the instructions on Activity Page 11C. Talk about the father's joy in welcoming his son home. God and the angels in heaven rejoice when we believe in Him.

Snack Time

Serve birthday cupcakes. Let the children add sprinkles. Also serve fruit kabobs with the leftover fruit from the "pig food." Let the children wear their party hats if they made them. Tell the children it's time for your party, and lead them in a prayer.

Live It Out

Have the children create their own rhyming book with illustrations (or have them draw pictures to illustrate the rhyming couplets of the Arch Book about the prodigal son or the action rhyme "The Prodigal Son" in *Wiggle & Wonder* (CPH, 22-3130). Take digital pictures of the illustrations, and make them into a PowerPoint slide "book." Show this for the Opening in Sunday School.

 **4 Closing** (5 minutes)

Going Home

What you do: Gather the take-home pages. Have CD and player ready.

Say   God is our loving and forgiving Father. He sent Jesus to be our Savior. He forgives us and gives us a home in heaven. Let's say "God is my loving, forgiving Father" together. Do so.

Sing   "Jesus Loves the Little Children" (*LOSP*, p. 94; CD 12) or "Have No Fear, Little Flock" (*LSB* 735; CD 1)

Pray   **Dear heavenly Father, You love us so much. Thank You for forgiving us when we say or do bad things. Thank You for sending Jesus to be our Savior. Amen.**

Reflection

During the puppet skits, did the children show an understanding of sin and God's forgiveness? In the coming weeks, look for ways to help the children say "I'm sorry" and "I forgive you" to one another.

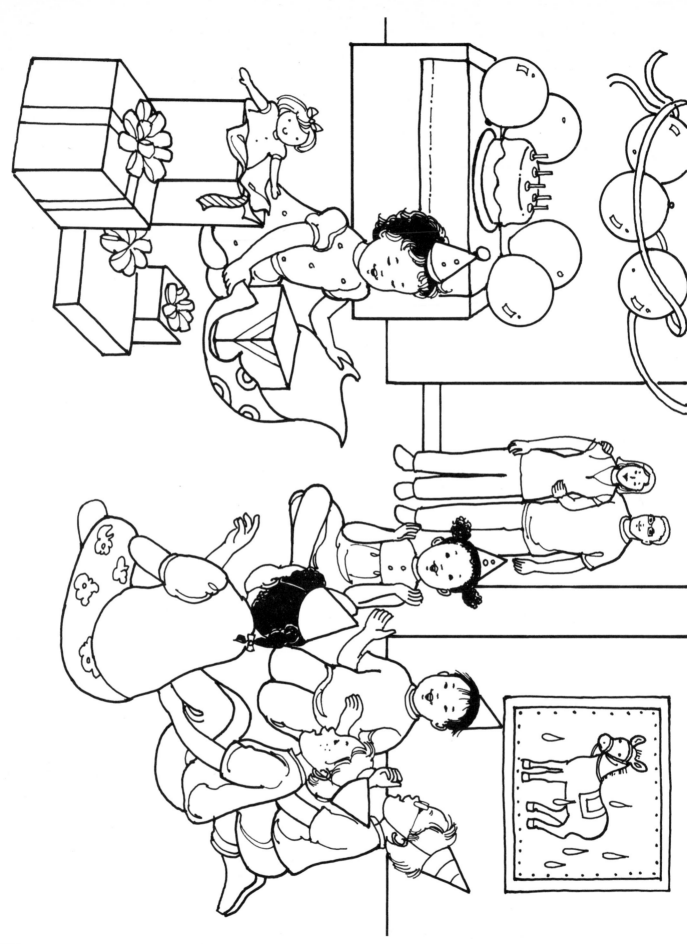

Activity Page 11A Growing in Christ® Early Childhood © 2007 Concordia Publishing House. Reproduced by permission. This page is available on the Teacher CD.

Activity Page 11B *Growing in Christ* Early Childhood © 2008 Concordia Publishing House. Reproduced by permission. This page is available on the Teacher CD.

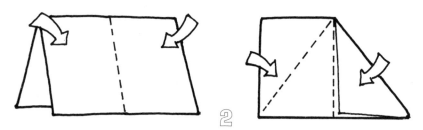

Fold corners forward until they touch in the middle.

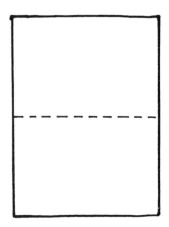

1 Fold an 8½ × 11-inch piece of paper in half horizontally.

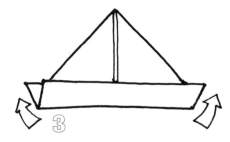

Fold the front bottom strip up over the triangular part on the front. Fold the back bottom strip up over the triangular part on the back.

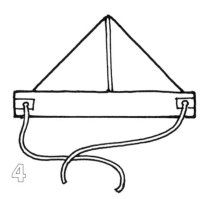

Overlap the ends of these folded strips and tape at the edges. Use a hole punch to make two holes at the corners. Attach a piece of ribbon or yarn through the holes for tying the hat on the child's head.

Provide crayons, glitter crayons, rickrack, pom-poms, tissue paper, and purchased stickers to decorate the hats. Talk about how God loves us and sent Jesus to be our Savior. That is Good News to celebrate!

Activity Page 11C Growing in Christ® Early Childhood © 2007 Concordia Publishing House. Reproduced by permission. This page is available on the Teacher CD.

Lesson 12

Preparing the Lesson

Date of Use

Jesus Heals Ten Lepers

Luke 17:11–19

Key Point

Jesus forgives and heals us from the sickness of sin and death. In faith, we respond with thankfulness.

Law/Gospel

Sin brought sickness and death into the world. **In His death and resurrection, Jesus heals me from the sickness of sin and overcomes death for me.**

Context

The healing of the ten lepers happened shortly before the crucifixion of Jesus, about AD 30. Going from Galilee "on the way to Jerusalem," Jesus goes as Prophet to announce and perform the fulfillment of the Law on the cross. He goes as Priest, the Son of God, to offer Himself in God's temple as a fit sacrifice on the cross for our sins. He goes as King to manifest the defeat of sin on the cross and in the tomb and to show forth His eternal Easter glory. He will face death like the prophets of old, yet He will rise from the dead as the firstfruits of our own resurrection and eternal glory.

Commentary

Sin, rejection, and death are universal. The lepers demonstrate this as a multiethnic group of Jews and at least one Samaritan. They may have had a number of infectious skin diseases; *leper* here has a wider meaning than leprosy proper, or Hansen's disease, the infectious bacterial disease affecting the skin, peripheral nerves, and upper airways of a person. These diseases led to a rotting of the flesh—an infectious living death that was perceived as the judgment of God upon the sin of people.

These ten lepers were outcasts, unclean, accursed, and forbidden to have the company of the healthy. Their lives prefigured the accursed loneliness of damnation, for there is neither honor among thieves nor fellowship among the condemned. The lepers could do nothing but call on Jesus and rely on His mercy alone. Their life was judgment; only Jesus could make a difference.

Paul tells us in Philippians 3:13–21 that those who hold true to Christ shall be vindicated by Him when they receive eternally glorious bodies, while those who are satisfied and comfortable here will come to naught. Sickness and health also fall into this eternal paradigm. Whereas all ten lepers receive the gift of healing, the Samaritan—the one despised as an "outsider"—returns. He who felt the judgment most keenly feels the deliverance most strongly. He does not take healing for granted.

We who suffer here shall know even greater joy in heaven. The more the world makes us suffer, the more joy Christ gives us in looking to our heavenly home because He first suffered for us and, having prevailed as the victor, stands with us in our suffering so that we may worship Him in glory.

To hear an in-depth discussion of this Bible account, visit cph.org/podcast and listen to our Seeds of Faith podcast each week.

Lesson 12

Jesus Heals Ten Lepers

Luke 17:11–19

Connections

Bible Words
I am the LORD, your healer.
Exodus 15:26

Faith Word
Thanks

Hymn
Have No Fear, Little Flock
(*LSB* 735; CD 1)

Catechism
Apostles' Creed: First and
Second Articles

Take-Home Point
God gives me a thankful
heart.

1 Opening (15 minutes)

Welcome Time

What you do: Before class, set up two activity areas. In one, put out copies of Activity Page 12A and crayons. Make copies of Activity Page Fun (below and on CD) for parents or classroom helpers. Adjust talk as necessary.

In the other activity area, set out medical supplies (e.g., a toy medical kit, Band-Aids, tissues, ice packs, empty pill bottles, slings, elastic bandages) and dolls.

Play the CD from your Teacher Tools. Greet the children, have them put their offering in the basket, and give them a sticker to put on the attendance chart.

Say Hi, [Colt], it's good to see you in Sunday School again. What did you do this week? Show interest in each child; then get child started in an activity.

Activity Page Fun Get a copy of Activity Page 12A. Show the Activity Page to your child. Talk about ways God cares for us when we are sick.

Say This child is sick. What do you think is wrong with him? Accept answers. When you are sick, what makes you feel better? The pictures at the top of the page show things that God uses to care for us and to help us to get better. They are also hidden in the big picture. Can you find them? Help your child find the hidden pictures.

Today, you will hear about ten men who had sores all over their bodies. These men were so sick that the doctors couldn't make them better. But Jesus could! Listen to find out what Jesus did. You can tell me about it later.

© 2016 Concordia Publishing House. Reproduced by permission. Available on the Teacher CD.

MATERIALS NEEDED

1 Opening	2 God Speaks	3 We Live	4 Closing
Teacher Tools Attendance chart & CD	**Student Pack** Lesson Leaflet 12 & sticker Craft Page 12	**Student Pack** Craft Page 12 Stickers	**Teacher Tools** CD
Student Pack Attendance stickers	**Other Supplies** Red dot stickers or red marker Paper-doll men or toy men Activity Pages 12B & 12C (TG, optional) *The Thankful Leper* Arch Book (optional)	**Other Supplies** Apple slices, cream cheese & raisins Activity Pages 12B & 12C (TG, optional) Paper Plus supplies (optional)	**Student Pack** Take-home materials
Other Supplies Activity Page 12A (TG) Medical supplies & dolls Resource Page 1 (TG, optional)			

Active Learning Encourage the children to pretend the dolls are sick and need to go to the doctor.

Say Today, you will hear about ten men who had sores all over their bodies. They asked Jesus for help. What do you think Jesus did?

Use your classroom signal when it is time to clean up. Sing a cleanup song (Resource Page 1). Cue the children to join you for the opening and story.

Sing Come and listen to God's Word, to God's Word, to God's Word. Come and listen to God's Word, from His book, the Bible.

Gathering in God's Name

What you do: Gather the children, and begin with this opening. To teach about the Church Year, use the materials in the Church Year Worship Kit.

Sing "God, Our Father, Hear Your Children" (*LOSP*, p. 14; CD 9) or another song

Invite the children to say the Invocation and Amen with you. Tell them "Amen" is the special word they get to say at the end of prayers and the like.

Begin In the name of the Father and of the Son and of the Holy Spirit. Amen.

Offering Have a child bring the offering basket forward. Sing an offering song.

Pray Thank You, God,*
for taking good care of us.*
You know everything we need.*
Thank You for sending Jesus*
to be our Savior.*
In His name we pray.*
Amen.*

*Have children echo each phrase at the asterisk.

Celebrate Birthdays, Baptism birthdays, and special occasions

2 God Speaks (20 minutes)

Story Clue

What you do: You will need Craft Page 12, red dot stickers or a red washable marker, and your Bible. Make a paper-doll chain of ten men using the Craft Page as a pattern, or cut out and assemble the men on the Craft Page using the directions in the Craft Time section. Open your Bible at the story, and put the men on top of it. *Option:* Use ten Little People or Lego figures, or the like.

Say God's Word, the Bible, tells us about some men who asked Jesus for help one day. Show chain of men or figures. **Let's count them.** Point to each man as you lead the children in counting to ten. **These ten men were very sick.** Place red marks on each paper person (if using figures, either do not mark them or have a wet wipe available to wash them off).

Jesus loved them. He was sad that they were sick. He wanted to help them. The men were too sick for the doctors to help, but they weren't too sick for Jesus! Let's listen to our story and find out what happened.

Bible Story Time

What you do: Have children do the actions with you as you tell the story. *Option:* Follow the directions on Activity Page 12B, and use the pictures on Activity Page 12C to make a story scroll or a storytelling tube. Or, read the Arch Book *The Thankful Leper* (CPH, 59-2212). Then have children act it out as you read it again. Video-record their dramatization and show it to them.

Say **One day, Jesus was walking to the big city of Jerusalem.** Have the children tap their hands on their legs or walk in place. **Near a small village, there were ten men who had bad sores all over their skin.** Have children count and hold up ten fingers, one at a time, or show the ten men on story scroll. **These men were very sick. They had a sickness called leprosy.**

The doctors could not make them better. Healthy people were afraid they would get sick too, so the sick men couldn't go near those who weren't sick. They couldn't go to see their families. They had to live by themselves outside their village.

The men knew Jesus healed people. They knew He could make them better. When Jesus got closer, the ten sick men called out, "Jesus, please help us! Please make us well!" Have children repeat words.

Jesus cared about the men. Show Jesus on the scroll or storytelling tube. **He said, "Go see the priests."** Priests were like our pastors. The priests were the ones who would decide if the men were healthy enough to go home to live with their families again. **So, the sick men started to walk to see the priests.** Have the children walk in place. **All at once, the sores on their skin went away!** Show the ten smiling men on scroll. **Jesus had healed them! They were so happy!**

One man went back to Jesus. Have the children hold up one finger. **Kneeling in front of Jesus, the man said, "Thank You for loving me and making me well. I know You are God's Son. I am so happy You made me better. Thank You!"** Show the kneeling man on scroll or tube. Have children kneel and say "Thank You."

Jesus healed the other nine men too. But they did not come back to say thank You to Jesus. Shake head no sadly. Roll the scroll or tube back to the Jesus picture. **Jesus was surprised. He asked, "Didn't I heal ten men? Where are the other nine?" Then Jesus looked at the man and said, "But I am glad you remembered to say thank You.** Show kneeling man again. **Go home. You believed in Me, and I have made you well."**

Jesus has power over sickness. He gives us doctors and medicine to help us when we are sick. But Jesus is the one who makes us better. The worst sickness Jesus has healed us from is our sin. Because Jesus died on the cross to pay for our sins, we know He loves us and is with us no matter what hurts we have. Because Jesus died for us, someday we can live with Jesus in a beautiful place called heaven, where there will be no more sickness or hurts. That makes me thankful! Show children on scroll or tube. **Let's say "Thank You, Jesus" together.**

Bible Story Review

What you do: Use Lesson Leaflet 12 to review the story. Then hand out the leaflets, the heart stickers, and crayons.

Key Point

Jesus forgives and heals us from the sickness of sin and death. In faith, we respond with thankfulness.

Ask **What was wrong with the men?** They were sick.

How many men did Jesus heal? Ten

How many said thank You? Just one

What are some things you are thankful for? Let children respond.

Have children count the number of sick men on your fingers as you lead them in the following action poem, or sing it to the tune of "Ten Little Indians."

Say **One sick, two sick, three sick men.**
Four sick, five sick, six sick men.
Seven sick, eight sick, nine sick men.
Ten men prayed to Jesus.

One sick, two sick, three sick men.
Four sick, five sick, six sick men.
Seven sick, eight sick, nine sick men.
Jesus made ten better.

One man, two men, three men left.
Four men, five men, six men left.
Seven men, eight men, nine men left.
Only one said thank You.

Give the children a sticker of a heart with a cross to add to the thankful man in the sidebar. Have children draw something they are thankful for in the box. On side 2, have them draw food, color the medicine, and connect the dots.

Bible Words

What you do: Read the Bible Words from Exodus 15:26 in your Bible: "I am the LORD, your healer."

Say **Jesus made the sick men better. He has power over sickness because Jesus is God. In the Bible, God says, "I am the LORD, your healer." God sent Jesus to be our Savior. The worst sickness Jesus has healed us from is our sin. Because Jesus died on the cross to pay for our sins, we know He loves us and is with us no matter what hurts we have. Because Jesus died for us, someday we can live with Jesus in heaven, where there will be no more sickness or hurts. Let's say our Bible Words together.** Lead children in the poem, and repeat the words with them several times.

Say **I open my Bible book up wide**
Hold your hands, palms together, in front of you.
And read the words that are inside.
Open your hands, keeping them together as an open book.
God says, "I am the LORD, your healer."

3 We Live (15 minutes)

Help children grow in their understanding of what the Bible story means for their lives. Choose the activities that work best with your class.

Growing through God's Word

What you do: Use the paper chain of ten men you made or Craft Page 12 (if you have an extra copy of it).

Say **Jesus loved the ten men** (hold up the paper chain of ten men)**. He healed all of them and made them better. Jesus loves us too. Jesus loves us when we're happy. Can you show me your smiling face?** Make smiling faces together. **Jesus loves us when we're sad.** Make sad faces together. **Jesus loves us when we're angry.** Make angry faces. **Jesus loves us when we're scared.** Make scared face. **He loves us when we are strong and healthy.** Lead children in flexing muscles. **He loves us when we are sick or feeling bad.** Put hand to head or stomach as if sick. **Jesus loves us, no matter what.**

Jesus takes care of us and gives us many wonderful things. Let's draw some things Jesus gives us that we are thankful for on the back of these men. Draw a simple picture of each thing the children suggest on the back of the paper chain of men (e.g., family, friends, food, pets, toys, answered prayers, health). Save the last cutout person.

Say **There are many things we can thank Jesus for. But sometimes, we are like the nine men who didn't thank Jesus. Sometimes, we don't say thank You either. But Jesus still loves us. He died on the cross to pay for our sins. Even when we don't feel thankful, Jesus still loves us. He helps us to be sorry for our sins. He forgives our sins and gives us a home with Him in heaven.** Draw a cross on the last cutout man with leprosy. **That is the best reason of all to tell Jesus thank You!** Lead the children in a prayer of thanks.

Craft Time

What you do: Give the children Craft Page 12, stickers, and crayons. To make the men into a chain, cut the page into two strips of five. Fold each strip back and forth, accordion style, so that there is only one showing. For easier cutting and so you don't cut off parts of the heads, do not cut too close to the men. Do the same with the other strip. Tape the strips together to make a strip of ten.

Option: Copy the Jesus figure on Activity Page 12B for each child. Children can color it, cut it out, and attach it to a craft stick or upside-down cup to make a puppet. Tell them to use their Jesus puppet and the ten sick men from the Craft Page to tell the story to those at home.

Ask **Who are these men? What is wrong with them?** Show the side with the sick men. **Let's add some more spots to show how sick they are.** Do so. **How many men does Jesus make better? Let's count them.** Do so. **Do you think the men are happy to be better?** Turn the men over to show ten smiling men. **Yes! How many men come back to thank Jesus?** Fold up the men so only one is left. **Just one.**

Have you ever been sick or sad? Accept answers. **You can talk to Jesus and tell Him how you feel. You can ask for help. Jesus hears our prayers. He promises that He will help us in a way that is best for us. Jesus gives us many things to be thankful for.** Unfold and turn the men over to the black and white side. **Let's think of some of Jesus' blessings.**

Use the stickers as prompts as you help the children identify some of

God's blessings (e.g., family, food, help when we are sick), and encourage the children to think of more things. They can put the stickers on the back of five of the men and color the remaining men. Some children may like to draw additional blessings on them (e.g., a friend's face, a pet, flowers). On the last man, have them draw a cross.

Say **God gives us many reasons to be thankful. We are especially thankful that Jesus died on the cross to pay for our sins. Let's draw a cross on the last man to show that.**

Paper Plus option: Use Activity Pages 12B and 12C to make a storytelling tube or scroll for each child. Follow the directions on Activity Page 12B.

Snack Time

Spread apple slices with flavored cream cheese. Let the children count ten raisins to add for smiles. Talk about how God gives us food to help us grow.

Live It Out

Pray for God's healing power. List sick people you and the children know. (You can find names on the prayer list in your church bulletin or website). Encourage children to pray for the people during the week. You can also thank God for His gifts by sharing them with others. Collect some gently used toys, books, and games to donate to a children's hospital, shelter, or agency that collects toys for refugee children.

 **4 Closing** (5 minutes)

Going Home

10, 1

What you do: Send take-home pages and crafts home with the children. Have your CD and CD player ready.

Say **Today, we heard how Jesus healed ten men who were very sick. Jesus forgives us and heals us too. One man returned to say thank You to Jesus. God gives us thankful hearts too, so we can praise Him. Let's say "God gives me a thankful heart" together.** Say this with the children.

Sing "Praise Him, Praise Him" (*LOSP,* p. 68), "God Takes Care of Us" (*S&W,* p. 48; CD 10), or "Have No Fear, Little Flock" (*LSB* 735; CD 1)

Pray **Dear Jesus,* You cared for the ten sick men* and healed them.* You love us too.* Help us* to be thankful* for all that You do,* especially for forgiving our sins.* Amen.***
Have the children echo the phrases at the asterisks.

Reflection

Did you help the children see that everything comes from God? In the coming weeks, how can you provide opportunities for them to respond in thankfulness and praise?

Find and circle these things in the picture. Talk about ways God cares for us when we are sick.

I am the LORD, your healer.
Exodus 15:26

Activity Page 12A Growing in Christ® Early Childhood © 2007 Concordia Publishing House. Scripture: ESV®. Reproduced by permission. This page is available on the Teacher CD.

The Ten Lepers

Luke 17:11–19

Jesus Figure

Copy, color, and cut out the figure of Jesus. Use Him with the ten lepers on Craft Page 12.

Story Scroll

To make a story scroll, enlarge and cut out the figures on Activity Page 12C, trimming the excess paper from each one. Cut a paper grocery bag to size to make a scroll, or tape several pieces of poster paper together. Tape the ends around wooden dowels or paper towel tubes. Tape the figures to the paper in order and roll in from the ends.

Start with the first picture. As you tell the story, keep unrolling to reveal each picture in order.

Storytelling Tube

Copy Activity Page 12C. Cut apart the strips and tape in order around a paper towel tube, so you can turn the strips independently as you tell the story to show the correct picture.

Activity Page 12B Art from *Show Me a Story.* Copyright © 2004 Concordia Publishing House.
Growing in Christ® Early Childhood © 2016 Concordia Publishing House. Reproduced by permission. This page is available on the Teacher CD.

Activity Page 12C Art © 2004 Concordia Publishing House.
Growing in Christ® Early Childhood © 2012 Concordia Publishing House. Reproduced by permission. This page is available on the Teacher CD.

Lesson 13

Preparing the Lesson

Jesus Blesses the Little Children

Mark 10:13–16

Key Point

Jesus welcomes us, who because of sin are like children—helpless, dependent, and needy—and blesses us with His love and eternal gifts.

Law/Gospel

In my sinful foolishness, I prize self-sufficiency and believe I can take care of myself, looking to the things of this world to satisfy and save me. **God knows that I am like a helpless child who can do nothing to save myself. In His love, He provides all that I need for this body and life, working salvation for me through His Son.**

Context

Following Jesus' discussion of marriage, adultery, and divorce early in the tenth chapter of his Gospel, Mark shifts into this story about parents and children. (Luke lowers the age even more: "Now they were bringing even infants to Him" [18:15].) Mark writes that the parents wanted Jesus to "touch them" (10:13), and Matthew records that the parents desired Jesus to "lay His hands on them and pray" (19:13).

In the following story about the rich young man who cannot say good-bye to his wealth (Mark 10:17–31), we see a stark contrast to these children. The young man won't let go of his reliance on worldly wealth, whereas the children receive Him who is the true God and Savior.

Commentary

Sinners do not run, walk, limp, or even crawl up to heaven's gates. They are carried there, as poor Lazarus was, by the angels (Luke 16:22).

The paralytic, lying on his mat, was carried to Jesus and let down through the roof by his friends (Luke 5:18–19). This is the model for how we come to our Lord (Mark 2:1–12). We are brought to Him, whether or not we realize it at the time.

So these infants and toddlers were brought to Jesus. Still today, the Father uses fathers and mothers to bring little children to Him, as parents (or others) bring children to the Divine Service and especially to Baptism. In a watery embrace, Jesus takes them in His arms, lays His pierced hands upon them, and blesses them with forgiveness and life. They cross into the kingdom of God through the river of the font.

This, however, is scandalous. Should we not allow children to grow up and make this decision on their own? Should they not be allowed to choose whether they want to be baptized and come to Jesus? Such are the objections of the world and of our flesh.

But as the Small Catechism says, "I believe that I cannot by my own reason or strength believe in Jesus Christ, my Lord, or come to Him; but the Holy Spirit has called me by the Gospel, enlightened me with His gifts, sanctified and kept me in the true faith" (Apostles' Creed, explanation of the Third Article).

The Lord chooses us, not we Him. He chooses children as emblems of the greatest in the kingdom of God because they can only receive from the God who loves to give. He brings them to Himself using parental hands and arms as His tools.

The disciples are looking up, as the world does, considering only some are important. So, they rebuke the people. They suppose Jesus is too busy, too important to hold snotty-nosed kids. But Jesus shows He came for all. He came to look down and gaze upon the helpless, the dependent, and the needy, and to bestow His love.

To hear an in-depth discussion of this Bible account, visit cph.org/podcast and listen to our Seeds of Faith podcast each week.

Catechism quotations: © 1986, 1991 CPH.

Lesson 13
Jesus Blesses the Little Children
Mark 10:13–16

Connections

Bible Words
[Jesus says,] "Let the children come to Me." Mark 10:14 (CD 4)

Faith Words
Bless, blessing

Hymn
Have No Fear, Little Flock (*LSB* 735; CD 1)

Catechism
Apostles' Creed: Second Article

Take-Home Point
Jesus loves me.

1 Opening (15 minutes)

Welcome Time

What you do: Before class, set up two activity areas. In one, put out copies of Activity Page 13 and crayons. Make copies of Activity Page Fun (below and on CD) for parents or classroom helpers. Adjust talk as necessary.

In the other activity area, provide a large piece of paper and magazines with pictures of children (parenting magazines often have multicultural children). Or find open source (free) online pictures of children in other countries, and print them on your home computer.

Play the CD from your Teacher Tools. Greet the children, have them put their offering in the basket, and give them a sticker to put on the attendance chart.

Say Hi, [Bella]. I'm glad you are here. Jesus loves you! He is glad you are here too. Show interest in each child; then get child started in an activity.

Activity Page Fun Get a copy of the Activity Page and crayons.

Ask Whom do you see in the picture? Does Jesus love the boy in the wheelchair? Does Jesus love the girl with glasses? Yes, Jesus loves all these children, no matter who they are. Point to child outline. **Can you make this child look like you? Jesus loves you too! Today, you will hear more about Jesus' love.** Have your child trace the dots. Read the Bible Words.

© 2016 Concordia Publishing House. Reproduced by permission. Available on the Teacher CD.

MATERIALS NEEDED

1 Opening	2 God Speaks	3 We Live	4 Closing
Teacher Tools Attendance chart & CD	**Teacher Tools** CD	**Teacher Tools** Craft Page 13 Stickers	**Teacher Tools** CD
Student Pack Attendance stickers	**Student Pack** Lesson Leaflet 13	**Other Supplies** Baby-care items Paper Plus supplies (optional)	**Student Pack** Take-home items
Other Supplies Activity Page 13 (TG) Magazines or pictures of children Dolls & baby items (optional) Resource Page 1 (TG, optional)	**Other Supplies** Mirror *Jesus Blesses the Children* Arch Book (optional)		

Active Learning Make a collage of children from all over the world. Have the children cut out the pictures you have supplied and glue them onto the paper.

Say **Look at all these children! God made every boy and girl in the whole world! Look how He made each child different!** Have children describe differences (hair color, eye color, big, small). **Jesus loves every boy and girl!**

Option: Set out dolls and baby items. Have the children pretend to feed and care for the "babies." Talk about how babies can't feed themselves or change themselves. They need big people to take care of them.

Say **In our Bible story today, some grown-ups bring babies and little children to Jesus. They want Jesus to bless the children and pray for them. Jesus loves children. Whether we are big or little, Jesus came to be our Savior. He forgives our sins and blesses us with His love.**

Use your classroom signal when it is time to clean up, or sing a cleanup song (Resource Page 1). Cue the children to join you.

Sing **Come and listen to God's Word, to God's Word, to God's Word. Come and listen to God's Word, from His book, the Bible.**

Gathering in God's Name

What you do: Begin with this opening. To teach about the Church Year, use the materials in the Church Year Worship Kit.

Sing "Jesus Loves the Little Children" (*LOSP*, p. 94; CD 12) or "Have No Fear, Little Flock" (*LSB* 735; CD 1)

Say **Jesus loves [Charlotte and José and Bella].** Name each child in your class. **Jesus loves all the children of the world. Today, you'll hear how Jesus told the little children to come to Him. He's glad you're here!**

Invite the children to say the Invocation and Amen with you. Tell them "Amen" is the special word they get to say at the end of prayers and the like.

Begin **In the name of the Father and of the Son and of the Holy Spirit. Amen.**

Offering Have a child bring the offering basket forward. Sing an offering song.

Pray **Dear God, we are small, but Your love is big. Thank You for loving each one of us. Thank You for being here with us today. Help us learn more about Your love. Amen.**

Celebrate Birthdays, Baptism birthdays, and special occasions

2 God Speaks (20 minutes)

Story Clue

What you do: Bring a mirror to show the children.

Ask **What do you see when you look in a mirror?** Let children comment as you do so. **When I look into this mirror, I see myself. I see the color of my hair. What color is it?** Let the children answer. **I see the color of my eyes. What color are they?** Let the children answer. Turn the mirror so the children can see their reflection in it. **What color hair do you have, [Kiara]? What color is your skin, [Hector]? What color are your eyes, [Nora]?**

Say God has made us all different, hasn't He? Do you think God loves some people more than others? Maybe He loves people with red hair more than people with brown hair. What do you think? Do you think He loves big people more than little children? Let's listen to our Bible story and find out.

Bible Story Time

What you do: Play the story on the CD (track 22), or tell the story using the following script. *Option:* Show the pictures in the Arch Book *Jesus Blesses the Children* (CPH, 59-1500) as you listen to or tell the story.

Show the children your Bible and tell them that this story comes from God's Word, the Bible. Everything in the Bible is true. God loves big people and little children. He wants all of them to know Jesus is their Savior.

Say **Jesus walked from town to town.** Walk in place. **Everywhere He went, Jesus taught people about God's love. He helped people with problems. He healed people who were sick. Many people came to hear Him talk. Many people came to Jesus for help. Jesus was very busy.**

One day, some moms and dads heard that Jesus was nearby. Cup hand around ear. **They wanted their children to see Jesus. So, they decided to bring their children to Jesus. They wanted Jesus to bless the children and pray for them.** Fold hands in prayer.

Some of the children said, "We're going to see Jesus!" Do you think they were excited to see Jesus? Some children probably ran ahead. Run in place. **Some dawdled and lagged behind. Some children, like the little babies, were probably carried by their moms and dads.** Pretend to carry baby in arms. **All of them could hardly wait to see Jesus.**

But when they got near, Jesus' disciples stopped them. Put up hand in stop motion and frown. **They said, "Go back home. Jesus is too busy to see children. He doesn't have time for you today." How do you think this made the children feel?**

But Jesus loved the children. Hug self. **He saw what happened. He wasn't too busy to see them.** Shake head no. **He came to be their Savior too. He told His disciples, "Let the children come to Me; do not stop them. My love and forgiveness are for children too."** Open arms wide. **Then, Jesus opened His arms wide and called the children to come to Him. They rushed up to Jesus, and He took them in His arms and blessed them.** Hug self.

Jesus loves us too. He knows we are sinful. He knows we need a Savior. He loves us so much that He died on the cross to be punished for our sins. He loves us so much that He came alive again so that those who believe in Him can go to heaven someday. He loves us so much that He calls us to come to Him through Baptism and His Word.

Jesus blesses us with His love and forgiveness. Jesus is never too busy for us. He always has time to help us. He always has time to listen to us when we pray to Him. He loves us no matter what.

Sing "Jesus Loves the Little Children" (*LOSP*, p. 94; CD 12)

Key Point

Jesus welcomes us, who because of sin are like children— helpless, dependent, and needy—and blesses us with His love and eternal gifts.

Bible Story Review

What you do: Hand out Lesson Leaflet 13 and crayons. Point to the Bible picture as you review the story using the questions. Then do the action rhyme (adapted from *Fingers Tell the Story*, p. 63) with the children.

Ask **What do you see in this picture?** Jesus, children and parents, disciples

What happened before what you see in the picture? Let children tell the sequence of story events: parents were bringing their children to Jesus so He could bless them; the disciples told them to go away; Jesus said let them come.

How do you think the children feel? Accept answers.

Say **Let's pretend we're the children going to see Jesus.** Have children stand up and do the actions with you.

"Let's go see Jesus," some grown-ups said one day.
Walk, walk, walk; walk, walk, walk.
Walk in place or around the room.
But Jesus' disciples said, "Stop, children. Go away.
"No, no, no; no, no, no."
Hold up hand and shake head no.
Jesus heard what they said; He told the children, "Don't go!
"Come, come, come; come, come, come."
Move arms in an inviting motion.
"I love children; I came to forgive everyone, you know."
Jesus loves us so; Jesus loves us so.
Use fingers to turn up corners of mouth into smile.

Have children sit down and turn to the sidebar sequencing activity on their leaflet. Do this with them, then have them complete the maze on side 2.

Bible Words

What you do: Open your Bible to Mark 10:14. Play words on CD (track 4).

Say **Our Bible Words today are the words that Jesus said to the children in the Bible story. Listen as I read them from God's Word.** Show the children where the words are in the Bible as you read them: **[Jesus says,] "Let the children come to Me."** Listen to the verse on the CD.

Jesus tells us this too. It doesn't matter how big or little we are. Jesus loves us all. He came to be our Savior. He forgives our sins. He always has time for us. He promises to hear our prayers and help us in a way that is best.

Talk about different times or situations in the children's lives and then ask if Jesus loves them. Have them say the Bible Words each time, starting with "Jesus says." For example,

Ask **Does Jesus love you when you fall and hurt yourself on the playground? Yes, Jesus says, "Let the children come to Me." Does Jesus love you when you are sick? Yes, Jesus says, "Let the children come to Me." Does Jesus love you when you are scared in the dark? Yes, Jesus says, "Let the children come to Me." Does Jesus love you when you have been naughty and need His forgiveness? Yes, Jesus says, "Let the children come to Me."** Have children say words with you or sing them with CD.

Teacher Tip

Young children love to hear the same story over and over. They learn vocabulary words and develop comprehension skills as they listen to, act out, or read the story. Studies also show that a major part of a child's language development occurs in the repetition of words and phrases. So be sure to include opportunities for review!

③ We Live (15 minutes)

Help children grow in their understanding of what the Bible story means for their lives. Choose the activities that work best with your class.

Growing through God's Word

What you do: Bring baby-care items (e.g., bottle, diaper, clothing) to show, and ask questions about the things babies need but cannot do for themselves. Write the children's answers on a large piece of paper.

Ask **Can babies feed themselves? Can they change their diapers or dress themselves? No, they need grown-ups to do all these things for them.**

You are getting bigger and bigger, so you can do many things on your own now. You don't drink from bottles anymore, do you? You don't wear diapers! There are lots of things you can do all by yourselves now.

Can you zip a zipper? color a picture? put on your shoes? Talk about other things children can do by themselves. **What are some things you still need help with? Can you tie your shoelaces? make your own food?**

Now that you are bigger, there some things you still need help with, but there are many things you can do by yourself. But no matter how big you get, there is one thing you can never do. Do you know what that is? You can never get to heaven by yourself. All of us—small or big, no matter who we are—need Jesus for that!

In our story today, Jesus said, "Let the children come to Me." Jesus knew that all of us say and do wrong things. We sin, but Jesus loves us, big or small. He came to be punished on the cross for our sins. He did that so we can go to heaven. After Jesus died and rose again, He went back to His Father in heaven. But someday, Jesus will come back to earth and take everyone who believes in Him to live with Him in heaven!

Jesus wants all people to believe in Him and trust in Him, just as little children do when they are baptized and know that He is their Savior. Forgiveness of sins and life with Jesus is the best blessing of all! Jesus also blesses us in many other ways. What are some ways Jesus loves and blesses you? Invite the children to share their thoughts.

Option: Have children line up in a row, one behind the other. You and a helper (or another child) hold your arms together like a drawbridge. Tell children to walk under the drawbridge. As they do this, sing the following song to the tune of "London Bridge." As each child walks forward, lower the bridge (your arms) and "catch" the child inside your arms. Help the child say the Bible Words to get out of the gate.

Active Learning Idea!

Sing **Heaven's gate is open wide, open wide, open wide.** *Put arms up.*
Heaven's gate is open wide; come meet Jesus.
Jesus loves you; yes, He does; yes, He does; yes, He does.
Lower arms around child.
Jesus loves you; yes, He does. He's our Savior.

Ask **What does Jesus say?** Help child say, [**Jesus says,**] **"Let the children come to Me."**

Growing in CHRIST.

Craft Time

What you do: Give the children Craft Page 13, stickers, and markers.

Cut the page on the solid line. Tape sections together. Fold on dotted lines to make an accordion book depicting children God loves.

Say **These children are from different countries. They speak a different language. They eat different food.**

Ask **Does God love them?** (Yes!) **What do you think their names are? What do they play with? What might they eat?**

Provide sticker hats. (It is okay if the children mix up the hats.) Have children make the blank child look like them by coloring the clothing and choosing a sticker hat to put on the child. Talk about how Jesus loves all the children and came to be the Savior of all.

Paper Plus option: Make the Craft Page into a mobile. Cut paper plates in half and write "Jesus Loves the Little Children" on each half. Give each child half a plate and decorating supplies (e.g., stickers, sequins, tissue). Cut the Craft Page children apart. Punch a hole at the top of each child and thread with yarn. Attach the children at varying lengths from the paper plate to make a mobile of children around the world.

Snack Time

Make finger Jell-O, and cut it into boy and girl shapes. Talk about friends and how Jesus is our Best Friend and Savior.

Live It Out

Encourage the children to ask a grown-up at home to help them find out more about the children pictured on their Craft Page and where they live, either in books or online. Tell them to pray for children in a different country each night, that they would come to hear of Jesus and His love too.

 **4 Closing** (5 minutes)

Going Home

What you do: Send home take-home pages and crafts. Cue CD.

Say **Jesus says, "Let the children come to Me." He loves us so much that He came to be our Savior. Let's say, "Jesus loves me" together.** Do so. **Now let's sing a song about that.**

Sing "Jesus Loves the Little Children" (*LOSP*, p. 94; CD 12), or watch preschoolers singing "Father Welcomes" on YouTube at www.youtube.com/watch?v=M0gZe_cTe8Y. Replay the video and sing along.

Pray **Dear Jesus, thank You for Your love. Thank You for taking away our sins and making us Your children. Amen.**

Reflection

Are you planning the right amount of activity? Feel free to pick and choose activities and modify them to work with your class.

[JESUS] says,

"Let the children come to Me." Mark 10:14

Activity Page 13 *Growing in Christ*® Early Childhood © 2008 Concordia Publishing House. Scripture: ESV®. Reproduced by permission. This page is available on the Teacher CD.

Songs & Wiggles-Out Rhymes

Movement is necessary to process and learn new information. Incorporate music and movement between periods of quieter learning to allow for this. Give children scarves or ribbon twirlers to use as they sing.

Songs

Cleanup Song
Tune: "Row, Row, Row Your Boat"
Clean, clean, clean the room.
Put our things away.
Hurry, hurry, hurry, hurry—
Then we'll sing and pray.

Gathering Song
Tune: "Are You Sleeping?"
Come with me. Come with me.
Be my friend. Be my friend.
Come and meet my Jesus.
Come and meet my Jesus.
He loves you. He loves you.

Welcome Song
Tune: "The Farmer in the Dell"
Jesus knows my name.
Jesus knows my name.
Jesus knows my name is [Jenna].
Jesus knows my name.

Toss a beanbag to the child whose turn it is to say or sing a name.

Birthday Song
Tune: "London Bridge"
We're so glad that you were born,
You were born, you were born.
We're so glad that you were born;
Thank You, Jesus!

Baptism Song
Tune: "Mary Had a Little Lamb"
God chose [Luke] to be His child,
Be His child, be His child.
God chose [Luke] to be His child,
Through Baptism and His Word.

Snack Song
Tune: "Jesus Loves Me, This I Know"
Thank You for the world so sweet,
Thank You for the food we eat,
Thank You for the birds that sing.
Thank You, God, for ev'rything.
Yes, how You love us! Yes, how you love us!
Yes, how you love us! The Bible tells us so.

Wiggles-Out Rhymes

Wiggles Out 1
Reach up high; now down low.
Sit like a pretzel—here we go!
It's time to close our mouths up tight
Turn finger like a lock over lips.
And listen with our ears—that's right!
Cup both ears.

Wiggles Out 2
Clap your hands for Jesus—1, 2, 3.
He loves you, and He loves me.
Stomp your feet for Jesus; He's our King.
He can protect us from anything!
Wave your arms for Jesus, to and fro.
He is with us wherever we go!
Hooray! *Clap and cheer.*

Getting Ready to Pray
Ten little fingers ready to play. *Wiggle fingers.*
Ten little fingers ready to pray. *Fold hands.*
Help me, dear Jesus, in every way *Bow head.*
To love and serve You every day. *Extend hands.*

Introducing the Bible Words
Here is my Bible.
Hold hands together, palms touching.
I will open it wide
Hold hands like an open book.
To read about Jesus
Point up.
From the words inside.
Pretend to read.

Going Home
Good-bye, good-bye, good-bye,
Wave.
Good-bye, my friends, to you.
Point to one another.
God bless you ev'rywhere you go,
Walk in place.
In all you say and do. Good-bye!
Wave.

Supply List

Every Week

Have a Bible, catechism, hymnal, children's songbook, offering basket, puppet, and CD player for use every week, as well as classroom supplies such as scissors, tape, glue, construction paper, stapler, hole punch, yarn or ribbon, and crayons or markers. Most lessons also include optional ideas using a tablet device, smartphone, or laptop.

Other Supplies

Many of these supplies are for Welcome Time or optional crafts. See each lesson to choose what you want to do; then highlight the supplies you'll need to get.

Lesson 1

- ❏ Play dough
- ❏ Jesus picture
- ❏ Grapes or fish crackers

Optional
- ❏ Embellishments
- ❏ Items that depict blessings

Lesson 2

- ❏ Brown, yellow & blue play dough
- ❏ Bird cookie cutters
- ❏ Seeds & plant
- ❏ Decorative bird & bird food
- ❏ Bag containing food, clothing, toys & additional items
- ❏ Newsprint
- ❏ Trail mix & gummy worms
- ❏ Pinecones, yarn, bird seed & shortening

Optional
- ❏ *Jesus Teaches Us Not to Worry* Arch Book

Lesson 3

- ❏ Cologne
- ❏ Scented items & cloth
- ❏ Gift box with cross inside
- ❏ Hand lotion
- ❏ Throw pillows
- ❏ Offering plate
- ❏ Paper heart
- ❏ 3 × 5 cards
- ❏ Popcorn, orange slices, or spice cookies

Lesson 4

- ❏ Toy baking utensils
- ❏ Play dough
- ❏ Picnic basket or lunch bag & snack
- ❏ Goldfish crackers
- ❏ Napkins & plastic sandwich bags

Optional
- ❏ Cake sprinkles, sequins
- ❏ Apron
- ❏ Go Fish card game
- ❏ *What's for Lunch?* Arch Book

Lesson 5

- ❏ Blankets or pillows
- ❏ Flashlight
- ❏ Paper or toy crown
- ❏ Sugar cookies or popcorn & popper

Optional
- ❏ Play dough with glitter
- ❏ *Jesus Shows His Glory* Arch Book

Lesson 6

- ❏ Toy people figures
- ❏ Colored paper
- ❏ Heart & cross cookie cutter or patterns
- ❏ Occupational items in bag
- ❏ Heavy paper or note card
- ❏ Trail mix & paper lunch bags

Optional
- ❏ O-shaped cereal or sandpaper

Lesson 7

- ❏ Paper & stencils of a heart & cross
- ❏ Soap, ointment, Band-Aids & gauze in story bag
- ❏ Shoebox & cups
- ❏ Cookie sheet & cornmeal
- ❏ Granola bars or trail mix & cups of water

Optional
- ❏ Play dough & heart & cross cookie cutters
- ❏ *The Story of the Good Samaritan* Arch Book

Lesson 8

- ❏ Cotton balls & glue stick
- ❏ Scarf or blindfold
- ❏ Bananas, coconut & plastic forks

Optional
- ❏ Tape recorder
- ❏ Toy animals & blocks
- ❏ *Jesus, My Good Shepherd* Arch Book

Lesson 9

- ❏ Communication devices & telephones
- ❏ Collage items

- ❏ Yarn
- ❏ Hug-shaped pretzels
- ❏ Paper strips

Optional
- ❏ Salt play dough
- ❏ *The Lord's Prayer* Arch Book

Lesson 10

- ❏ Magnets & magnetic items
- ❏ Pretzel sticks or crackers & pressurized cheese

Optional
- ❏ Dead plant
- ❏ *Get Up, Lazarus!* Arch Book
- ❏ *What Happened When Grandma Died?*

Lesson 11

- ❏ Fruit, bowls & knife
- ❏ Story bag with party favors
- ❏ Paper plates & paper cups
- ❏ Cupcakes & sprinkles

Optional
- ❏ Dishpan of sand & toy pigs
- ❏ *The Parable of the Prodigal Son* Arch Book
- ❏ Yarn or ribbon

Lesson 12

- ❏ Medical supplies & dolls
- ❏ Red dot stickers or red marker
- ❏ Paper-doll men or toy figures
- ❏ Apple slices, cream cheese & raisins

Optional
- ❏ *The Thankful Leper* Arch Book

Lesson 13

- ❏ Magazines or pictures of children
- ❏ Mirror & baby-care items
- ❏ Finger Jell-O cut in shape of children

Optional
- ❏ Dolls, baby items & paper plates
- ❏ *Jesus Blesses the Children* Arch Book

Supply List Growing in Christ® Early Childhood © 2016 Concordia Publishing House. Reproduced by permission. This page is available on the Teacher CD.